GETTING REAL WITH GOD

HOW TO FIND PEACE WITH A PAINFUL PAST

ANNAMARIE ALTOMARE

HIGH BRIDGE BOOKS
HOUSTON

Getting Real with God
by Annamarie Altomare

Copyright © 2023 Annamarie Altomare

Printed in the United States of America
ISBN (Paperback): 978-1-954943-65-0
ISBN (Hardcover): 978-1-954943-66-7

High Bridge Books titles may be purchased in bulk for educational, business, fundraising, or sales promotional use. For information, please contact High Bridge Books via www.HighBridgeBooks.com/contact.

Published in Houston, Texas, by High Bridge Books.

Photography by Tammy Turk.

For all women at the well.

CONTENTS

Introduction and Letter from the Author

I REMEMBER WHEN, AS A YOUNG SOLDIER IN THE ARMY (I was 22 years old), I had a blast of anger in the presence of my platoon sergeant. I had worked a 10-hour overnight shift and was notified right before I finished my shift that I had a 9 a.m. meeting at the human resources center to review my promotion packet for the coming year. At the time, I was an E-4/specialist and had done all the required work to be promoted to sergeant. Although I had not planned this meeting, it was not unreasonable to be called in for review or to sign paperwork. The message came via my chain of command, and coming off from such a long overnight shift, I was irritated that my sleep would be interrupted.

I had not yet discovered the joys of coffee, so I was super cranky and not quite user-friendly. I went to the meeting after getting off duty at 8 a.m., and finally, after two hours of waiting, I met with the HR person. She looked everywhere for my file but did not find it and sent me away empty-handed. I was furious by the time I made it back to my barracks building. I saw my platoon sergeant down the hall and made a beeline for him. We went into his office, where I chastised him up one side and down the other for sending me to a meeting after an overnight shift, only to find that the person I was told to meet with could not locate whatever documents I needed to review and had sent me away empty-handed. I was so angry, and I read him the riot act, losing my temper even though he did not deserve it. He was gracious about my temper tantrum, which made me even more irritated.

I went to my barracks room and finally got some much-needed sleep. I had to report for duty that evening to work the same overnight shift again and showed up to formation still groggy and a little cranky. My platoon sergeant called me to his office after formation. I immediately thought the worst... that I was receiving a reprimand for my outburst earlier that day, which I deserved. I had a pit in my stomach; it made my heart race, my skin hot, and left me so nervous that I could barely focus. I made a feeble attempt to justify my outburst to my supervisor, but he cut me off and asked that I remain silent. He then proceeded to tell me that, after I left him that morning, he made inquiries as to who scheduled the appointment and why they sent me away after not finding my file. My platoon sergeant smiled and told me that they did not locate the file because I had made the cutoff scores for promotion, meaning I had been promoted to the rank of sergeant, and that my file had already been sent up my chain of command for confirmation.

I was stunned. Speechless at the news. Embarrassed that I had made such a fool of myself. Shocked that I was so clueless. I owned up to my earlier outburst and apologized profusely to him. He accepted my apology, congratulated me, and just like that, the slate was wiped clean. Not only had I been forgiven of my earlier tantrum, but I was also given a promotion. I kicked myself for days in agony because of how rude and unprofessional I was to my platoon sergeant. I knew better, and I found it very difficult to forgive myself for acting so irrationally, venting my anger on my boss. Like most women, I spent hours wallowing in self-pity, overthinking, and overanalyzing every detail. I replayed it in my head, imagining how I could have handled things better, trying to be worthy of the promotion the army had given me. No amount of apologizing to the universe was going to make it better because, after all, my boss had already forgiven me. Why couldn't I just forgive myself and move on?

I couldn't do that until I owned up with God about what I had done. I had to swallow my pride and receive my promotion in humility. Despite being in the wrong, I stood in formation and received my new rank in front of my superiors, peers, and subordinates. I realized that I had to do the difficult thing and accept accountability for my actions, which had not been acceptable. I had to "take my lumps," forgive myself, and move on.

In any relationship, whether friend, betrothed, parental, business, etc., holding yourself accountable for your own actions, or "owning up," is key, especially if you want your relationships to last and grow. This process is called taking ownership.

In my relationship with God, owning up is even more significant. After all, He already knew what my actions would be, and He forgave me anyway. The difficult part is loving and forgiving myself. He loves you too, and He is ready and willing to forgive and pour abundant blessings on you and me. Romans 3:23 says that "all have sinned and fall short of the glory of God." This scripture means that, at one time or another, every one of us has done something similar in nature to what I did when I had my angry outburst with my supervisor: sin.

You may not ever lose your temper like I did, but instead, maybe you hide your feelings and cuss people out when they're not around you. Perhaps you deal with jealousy, greed, alcohol, drugs, sex, or materialism, all of which are accompanied by any number of equally vexing behaviors. The problem with never owning up is that the guilt you and I carry lives in our minds, in a small closet with brick walls, no windows, and a locked door. We keep that closet neat and tidy so the world can't see it. But these guilty thoughts, or skeletons, come out of that closet at the worst times, constantly reminding us of our mistakes, our bad decisions, actions that we are ashamed of, and words we spoke in anger that caused hurt to someone else. That closet not only keeps us locked in, but more importantly, it also keeps God locked out. It puts limits on our relationship with God, which, in turn, limits how He can bless us.

We are His children, but being unable to face God because we are busy hiding what we did from Him is not a free or victorious lifestyle. We get to a point where we believe we are beyond help, that we do not need to bother God with every detail because we are too far gone and dirty, thinking that we must be clean before we can even approach Him. This limits our relationship with Him and keeps us in mediocrity. The thing is, He knew your "secret," your decision, your actions, or inactions before you even did it—and He still loved you anyway.

I believe that guilt is the main issue that holds people back from their purpose. Not taking ownership of our actions is like living with a layer of plastic wrap over our minds. Maybe you can't see it, but it restrains your thought life every time you try to live in your blessing because the guilt is also trapped under the plastic wrap. Every time life presents a happy moment, you and I quickly move to "self-sabotage" mode because deep down, we are still beating ourselves over the head because of some dark secret(s) in our past and we believe we are not worth the blessing. Today, this self-hate cycle continues to rule over people everywhere. It keeps you and me from living in the blessings that God has for us. It also makes certain that we never really uncover our purpose, that we stay comfortable in mediocrity instead of becoming everything God intended us to be.

God has forgiven you and me, but when we refuse to accept His forgiveness and continue to walk around as though He hasn't, spending precious time overthinking and over-analyzing the issue, then we are preventing God from blessing us. Instead of wearing His blessings, we wear our guilt and self-pity. He already chose you and me, even while we were still sinning. Because of His grace, we can hang up our "victim here" t-shirt and instead wear the blessings and favor God has for us. Walking in God's blessings and favor will not protect you from the attacks of the enemy, but it does give you a fighting chance of living through those attacks and remaining in God's peace and calm.

Why did I write this book? We all have a fallen, sinful nature. No matter how much we want to do good, we each have something that keeps us trapped in guilt and shame. We might be able to lie to others about our issues and keep hiding our skeletons in our closets, continuing to successfully fool people for years. But if you and I are part of the Body of Christ, the Holy Spirit will convict us. The key is in our willingness to be obedient to the Holy Spirit's convictions and resolve the hidden issue with God. Until we get to the point of being humbled, like I did when I had my angry outburst at my supervisor, we are destined to stay in that small brick closet with no way of escape, except through Jesus, who holds the key.

Owning-up and apologizing, or "taking our lumps" for our actions, is critical to living a victorious life. We may lose everything in the process of getting real, making one bad decision after another. The consequences of our actions can sometimes be quite severe. You may lose your spouse, your home, your vehicle, custody of your children, and your job; you may even end up in jail. But God promises to bless you through the storm. He will give you beauty for those ashes. Whatever the enemy uses to harm you, God will use it for your good. Because of our own choices and subsequent behavior, we need to come clean with God if we really want to live in the freedom Christ has for us. This is the first and most critical step to living a victory-filled life.

Your sin, and mine, can be made manifest in any number of addictions or destructive behaviors—liquor, drugs, nicotine, pornography, sex, uncontrolled spending, gambling, tax evasion, social media, gaming, you name it. If it takes the throne in your mind, meaning you put that thing first, you are making a conscious choice to turn away from God, not the other way around. The guilt that results from our participation in those destructive activities draws us even further away from God; that is how the enemy keeps you and I enslaved, and eventually we become indifferent to God, believing that while we are basically good people, we are too dirty, too far gone for God to care.

There is victory on the horizon for you and me. Being saved does not automatically recreate you or me into a perfect person. Yes, you are a new creation in Christ when you accept Him as your Lord and Savior, and you are made perfect *in* Him. However, our bad habits, desires in our hearts, and our sin nature will pull us back into the abyss in a hot second if we give way to temptation or distraction. Countless Christians, sons and daughters of the Most High God, have freedom in Christ, but because of the skeletons in the closet that have not yet been resolved, we still choose to live in mediocrity. We do not understand that we can choose to give these issues to God instead of living in guilt and shame, which overshadows our innermost being. I wrote this book to help guide you to your healing and mentor you to victory. We will dive deep into the hallmarks of living in guilt and how to lay them to rest at Jesus' feet. Although we have salvation, brokenness still comes in all shapes and sizes. Depression, suicidal thoughts, addiction, broken heart, broken body, and your dirtiest, darkest sex secrets were all already known to the Father *before* you were saved.

The enemy will use your guilt against you, reminding you of that bad decision, those hurtful words you spoke to your spouse or children. You can get free from those self-destructive behaviors, and in *Getting Real with God*, it is my prayer that you receive the gift of a victorious, abundant life in Christ by applying the tools found in this book.

He chose you, even while you were still sinning; now it's your turn to choose Him.

In Christ,

Annamarie Altomare

PART 1
IDENTITY IN CRISIS

1

WHO ARE YOU?

A fool vents all his feelings, but a wise man holds them back.

—Proverbs 29:11

AS MUCH AS I HATE TO ADMIT IT, I WAS A FOOL. I WASTED years of my life trying to prove myself to my mother, my father, and my extended family. Trying to prove that I was somebody worth something, that I had value. In reality, I was trying to figure out my identity, not really understanding who I was or if I even had a purpose for living. I had been angry as a teenager and became toxic as an adult. I was lost, godless, angry at the world for the hand I'd been dealt, ready to whip out my victim card at the slightest notice when things weren't going my way.

How did I get this way? I was a victim of child abuse and sexually assaulted by a family member as a teenager. When I did finally leave home to join the army, my freedom was quickly revoked by the horror of sexual harassment on steroids that I lived in at my first duty station in the Army. I was more than angry; I was self-righteous and contentious, and I allowed my anger to be my addiction and my fuel for years.

There are young girls, young women, and even old women out there who have been through what I've been through, and some women have been hurt even more deeply than I was. There are women out there who have been where I have been and who hide the same things that I hid. There are women out there looking for forgiveness in a world that is so cold, negative, judgmental, and unforgiving that they dare not speak of their shame. I know that you are out there. And I know it is for you that I am sharing my story. God wants you to know that it is not over, you are not trash, and you are not an outcast. God wants you to know that He is not done with you yet and that your pain will not be wasted.

Spend five minutes on any news outlet or social media feed and witness the countless results or consequences of angry, prideful, broken people unable to control their emotions, not understanding that their actions cause collateral damage to others, whether intended or not. But how did they get that way? Where in a person's life does the moral compass lose its azimuth?

When you were growing up, what factors in your life had a bearing on your decisions? Did you even know who God was? Did outside influences encourage you to make bad decisions? Did you know if your actions hurt God? And if you did get off course, what brought you back to God?

I didn't just get off course—I made a whole new path entirely constructed of my response to all the wrongs I had lived through. Here is my story.

As a young child, I was innocent, relying on my parents and family to love me, teach me, and raise me while trusting their guidance and leadership. I needed reassurance, confidence, and love from my parents, and I yearned for their approval my whole life, but it never came. Where most kids are safe and happy in their childhoods, I lived as a subject to the harsh realities of child abuse; my earliest memory is of my birth father attempting to end my life. I was two years old at the time. My parents divorced when I was just a year old, so my relationship with my dad never took root. My parents were fighting, and I remember crying, screaming more like. I'm not sure if it was his frustration and anger with me or mom, probably a combination of both, but my dad picked me up and threw me across the room. The cast iron radiator broke my fall when my head landed on it, leaving me bleeding from the back of my head. I remember my mom having to hitchhike to get me to the emergency room because my dad left the premises right after he threw me, driving off in the only car we had.

My dad's mother, Elsie, a woman I've never referred to as a grandmother, took care of my older brother and me when our mom was at work. She lived in a 1950's bungalow in Denver. Elsie would lock me in her hallway closet, where she kept her Hoover vacuum. At breakfast, I would get cereal and then spend the day in the closet. My brother, on the other hand, would get steak and eggs and spend the day watching TV with Elsie. She loved my brother, but me not so much. My mother used to tell me that Elsie loved her boys (my dad had three brothers) but hated my mother, and that hate trickled down to me. So, the vacuum closet is where I spent much of the early years of my childhood, with my stuffed bunny for company. My mom would pick us up after work and take us home, but there was never any mention of the closet.

The next time I saw my dad, I was 13 and well beyond my mother's control. She sent me to live with my dad and his second wife, Kelly. Unfortunately, it only lasted six months, but in those six months away from my mom, I learned that my dad was a police officer. I never knew that growing up, but seeing his uniform for the first time, I was intrigued. My dad would show me a bunch of old crime scene photos of homicides mostly. It was our only bonding experience, and I knew then that I wanted to be a police officer too. But I was also very reckless and rebellious, and it would be another 20 years before that dream came to life.

At the age of 13, my relationship with my mother hit a wall. I knew at this point that she was going through my things, and

I'm still not sure why. Nevertheless, I wrote a fictitious diary and hid it in my dresser. Several days later, she confronted me about the diary, which proved to me that she was going through my things. She called my dad and asked him to take me for a while because she could no longer cope.

I stayed with my dad for about six months before returning to my mother's house. I'm not exactly sure why I went back to my mom's house, but I am certain that I probably made my step-mother's life difficult. She was trying to raise a young family and I didn't quite fit in. Nothing against her—she's a wonderful woman, but back then, I was beyond her help. I was too angry and unwilling to let anybody in. The only bonding I had with my stepmother was when I turned 14 and started blossoming. She was gracious and helpful.

My mom and stepdad were still at odds and separated, so going home was bearable for a while. Then they made amends, and my stepdad moved back into the house. It was all fine at first, at least until I woke up to my stepdad groping me multiple times in the middle of the night, but I could never summon up the courage to tell my mother. I was more afraid that she would side with my stepdad the same way she chose him over my older brother, Joseph. Joseph and my stepdad didn't get along, and eventually, my brother ran away when I was 11. He was only 14 when he started a street gang with some of his friends and to this day still runs with them. He had been gone three years before the sexual assaults started.

There was no God in my childhood home. There was drug use, drinking, and my mother's revolving door of boyfriends before she met the man who she eventually married. I was eight years old when I met my stepdad, the morning after she had met him at a bar, and my mom married him about three months later. For a while, things got a little better with a stepdad in the house. Mom was a little less party and a little more stay-at-home. It was nice for a while. I turned into an "A" student and even sang in the choir at school. I played some sports, mostly volleyball, but singing had become my favorite thing to do.

But then the fighting began and never seemed to stop. I had a hard time with the yelling and things getting broken. After the sexual assaults started, I became more and more angry at my environment. When I was 15, I started to sneak out of the house whenever my mom and stepdad would fight, climbing out of my bedroom window to escape the fallout. I never went anywhere in particular, just walked around for an hour or two and returned when the house was dark and all had gone to bed.

Eventually, at 16, I followed my brother's example and ran away with no plan, no clue, and no purpose. I ran away on two separate occasions. My first attempt was an epic failure, as I went to live with my then-boyfriend, a decision that turned out to be a huge mistake. While living with him, I had gotten pregnant, and my boyfriend made it very clear that he did not want a baby. He became physically abusive over the matter. I'm not going to justify my decisions or debate the Roe v. Wade battle with you. I had an abortion. And yes, it was an extremely difficult and painful experience on every level. For women who might be considering this as an option in their life, be warned … it's not all smooth sailing. The counselors don't tell you about the room you are in during the procedure. They don't warn you about the physical pain of having a child removed from your womb or the emotional pain and anguish, the veil of shame you live with every single day, the way it decimates your insides with searing pain all while looking at the ceiling at a picture of a beautiful hot air balloon.

The second time I ran away, I dropped out of school. I was still 16 and had enough of the bullying that was happening in my own home. My grandmother, Grandma Maddie (she was my mom's mom), was so wonderful to me. She was an oasis of calm and non-judgment in the storm that was my life. She took me in, and I stayed with her for the remainder of the school year. She enrolled me in a school district where she lived, and somehow the news of my sexual promiscuity and poor decisions had reached that school. I remember feeling like an outcast—judged, unwelcome, and unwanted. One day during lunch, I was leaving the cafeteria to go outside. As soon as I stepped out of the door, another student closed the door behind me, and my fellow classmates all gathered in a circle blocking any possibility of an exit. "Whore" they chanted and yelled repeatedly, not allowing me to leave.

When I finally did break through them, I ran as fast and as hard as I could back to my grandmother's house. I had been so scared and so traumatized that I peed my pants, literally. I never went back to that school. Not even to get my property from my locker. I dropped out of school, although I never told my grandmother what happened. In fact, I've never mentioned it, and until now, the only person who knew any of this was my best friend, Ann.

Thinking about Grandma Maddie brings back wonderful memories of being safe, spending hours creating and painting ceramics together and eating her homemade empanadas. Where the rest of the planet had let me down, Grandma Maddie lifted me up. I never wanted to leave her—she was always so genuine to me and was interested in me as a person. She was the only person I knew who never wanted anything from me in return, never asked me for money, never put conditions on our relationship. I lived with her until my great-grandfather forced my mother to take me home, right before my 17th birthday. Great-grandpa Joe was old-school; he believed I belonged with my mother and that it was her responsibility to raise me.

My mother and grandmother had such a terrible relationship. My mother had a lot of issues with my grandmother, blaming my grandma for things that happened when my mom was growing up. She blamed my grandma for being a drunk and for never being home when her siblings were growing up. I know grandma was far from perfect, but I don't recall seeing excessive drinking. She only had one bottle of vodka in the house, but she rarely touched it.

My mother was angry that she was the oldest of grandma's children and, by default, became the caretaker of her four siblings. I'm not certain if they ever reconciled. My Grandma Maddie passed away years later while I was still in Germany in the army. My mother waited for three years before she told me about my grandma's passing. I was crushed.

Going back to my mother's house meant living with my mom and stepdad and going back to school. I was so afraid of people at that point. I became a doormat, always intimidated by people, and I never really knew who I was. My identity crisis had been firmly intact before I could even talk. From the time I was born, I had the same issue that plagues millions of other fatherless children: who am I? In contrast to my personality, I became incredibly introverted and buried my head in books, helping me temporarily escape my life. Like a dog that experiences patterns of abuse at the hands of its owners and then becomes reluctant to trust people, I wanted to trust and be around people but found it extremely difficult. I buried my thoughts, feelings, opinions, personality, and anger, being agreeable always and never rocking the boat. There is nothing more destructive than an angry doormat.

I went back to high school that same year and graduated two years later. I had to go through a counseling session with Dr. P. Campbell—the woman I credit with turning me around—who not only challenged me to turn away from the path that I was on but also believed that I *could* turn away, that I had what it took to make a success of my life. She believed in me when I could not believe in myself. At her challenge, I graduated from high school with a 3.6 grade point average. I often think of her and give thanks to God for her influence on my life. I hate to think how different my life would have been without her intervention.

Like most teens, I had to find a job, but where most teens want the extra money, I wanted a way to escape my house. I found a job with a home improvement company as a cashier and worked there until I graduated high school and left for the army. It kept me out of the house every evening and weekend. My stepfather stopped making advances on me, but my mother and I fought about everything. I became silent, just agreeing and doing my chores. Speaking up for myself and having my own voice was not allowed. Going to school and work were my breathing space, and I purposefully worked every night because it was my home evasion plan. We were at odds with each other, so working every night after school and coming home at bedtime was my way of avoiding further confrontation. I did my homework during my breaks at work.

In my senior year, I met and thought I fell in love with another high school student who was also a senior, Louis. We took the long way of getting to know each other and maintained a healthy friendship prior to becoming intimate. I knew his mother; he knew my parents. I thought we were a good match, and it was all coming together quite well.

All was well right up until I got pregnant again. That is when I learned that Louis had already fathered one child who was two years old at the time and that he, in no uncertain terms, was not willing to father a second child. He had kept his firstborn a secret from me. Graduation was just over a month away. To my disgrace and shame, I had a second abortion. Some say it's the easy way out, but in all honesty, it is the worst thing I could ever have done. Years later, when I did meet the man that I was to marry and conceived a child with him, I miscarried. And the death of that child was monumental. I believed that God was passing judgment on me for having taken the lives of two innocent.

I had signed on with the US Army at the beginning of my senior year in high school on the delayed entry program and left for basic training a few months after I graduated. I needed autonomy, and I needed to figure out who I was without my mother telling me who I was.

For me, basic training was not very difficult. Get up early, get yelled at all day long, and do what they tell you. It was just like being at home, so the transition was easy for me. I joined the Military Police Corps, and completed all my training in Alabama. I ended up going to Germany, which I loved. With its endless castles and world history in every direction, I was full of optimism, excitement, and adventure. France was so close I could almost taste the croissants and fine wines. Unfortunately, I was sent to a remote site called Kriegsfeld, but I have always referred to it as Hell.

My first duty station was a place that the army kept secret; at least, I wish it was kept secret and that I'd been spared from having gone there. The duty station had about 800 soldiers, and maybe 30 of us were women. In the 80s, women were not needed or wanted in a remote site, among the ranks of MPs. As an angry doormat, I tried my best to be invisible; after all, it worked well at my mother's house. In the military, however, it works exactly the opposite; being a doormat made me a bigger target. Sexual harassment in the 80s happened a lot. But back then, protection from it was not yet a thing, so it was open season on us gals. Quite a few of the men in my duty station were foul, vulgar, and nasty. They didn't want women among their ranks, and they made that point very clear to me from day one. This was a place for men, where women were treated as party favors, not soldiers.

We worked in an area that was hidden from the public, a place called "the hill." The job itself was straightforward and worthwhile; however, living and working among wolves made every day a challenge. We worked 24 hours on, 24 hours off, on a two-week rotational basis. During our on-duty hours, we would rotate shifts but were not allowed to leave the hill during our on-duty hours, meaning once you were there, you were locked in for the full 24 hours.

We had one television with only one channel—this was before satellite TV was in the open market. The guys would bring VHS movies to the common room, where we all stayed during down time. The room was in a large uninspired government facility where everything from floor tile to drop ceilings were shades of beige. We had a large screen projector-type TV, a pool table, a kitchen where the chow hall would bring our food to us for every meal, a table where we played cards, and two sleep rooms with bunk beds in them. I never felt safe in the bunk rooms, so I always stayed clear of them, preferring to stay in the open areas where I felt safer.

The guys would bring a wide variety of pornographic movies to the common room. And by variety, I mean disgusting stuff that involved all sorts of filth. Since the only place to escape the videos was the kitchen, that's where I stayed in my down time, playing cards with the guys who also preferred not to watch what was on the TV screen.

At first, their lewd comments and suggestions were shocking to me, but I quickly learned that their behavior would never be corrected and that they were free to conduct themselves however they wanted. My squad leader was one of the worst, a constant disappointment in the rank he held. As an E-6 staff sergeant, he was responsible for leading me, teaching me, and helping me grow and promote. Instead, he kept telling me that life would be much easier for me if I would just cooperate with him, give him a little nookie here and there, and he would make all the problems go away. I found it difficult to respect him when he would ask me to give him a blowjob…that he would make things easier for me if I would comply.

Accountability was virtually nonexistent for several reasons, including an influential person in our chain of command who was gay. In the 80s, in the army, you could be put out for that lifestyle. The lack of supervision was a direct result of soldiers who knew about this person and used his secret to leverage whatever they wanted.

I still have a hard time talking about some of their activities because of the criminal acts they got away with. I remember being on the third floor of the male barracks building. I was walking down the hall when I heard a strange sound. My curiosity got the better of me as I looked for the source of the noise. As I came nearer to the room where the noise was coming from, I saw that the door was slightly ajar. I heard the noise again. I inched to the door and pushed it open. I saw a young naked German woman tied with rope to a barracks bed. There were several soldiers in the room taking turns with her. The look in her eyes was unforgettable and continues to haunt me, even now as I remember it.

Fear washed over me and paralyzed me to the spot I stood in as I watched what they were doing to her. One of the soldiers in the room came to the door, stood over me, and said, "Walk away, Lopez, or you're next."

I ran away as fast as I could, not helping her, not reporting it. I felt like such a coward, running away like a scare little girl. I was afraid that I would be next. That fear immobilized me and kept me in silence. I felt so angry that my newfound freedom away from my mother's house was taken away from me by men who were supposed to be military police. I felt like I had graduated from one prison to another.

Eventually, I reached my tipping point after being there for about nine months. I was in the common room on the hill when one of the guys put a porn movie in the VHS player. I got up to leave the room when one of the guys grabbed me on my right butt cheek in an aggressive and menacing manner. I turned toward him with every ounce of anger in me and hammer-fisted his nose, breaking it. I followed it up by putting the tip of my nose to his and then quietly told him that I would kill him if he ever touched me again. And no, I was not kind or nice when I said it; on the contrary, I meant every word.

It was so silent in that room that you could have heard a pin drop. They were shocked to see me fight back since they were so used to getting their way with everybody else.

I didn't get in trouble for breaking that guy's nose, although I should have. Instead, I was sent away to another duty station in Germany near the border of France. Whether it was for my safety or theirs, I'll never really know — probably both. Up to that point, I had endured hatred on a level no person should ever be subjected to. It was also there that the warrior in me broke out of the closet. Quite literally, hitting that soldier in the face like that was my fight-or-flight response to all my tormentors' innuendoes, remarks, and physical advances. Freeze no longer existed in me. I decided that if I was going to become a victim, I was going to take body parts with me.

But it didn't end there. The place that I was sent to was beautiful and quite close to the border of France. I worked with a Protective Services Division at that time, learning how to drive cars fast and evasively. I even got to drive a hard car, which is an armored-plated car with bullet-resistant glass throughout. It was one of the better highlights of being in Germany. I had a whole new group of friends, and there were a lot more women stationed there, so it was a lot of fun. Our barracks building was co-ed, so men and women lived on every floor, kind of like a college dorm.

I enjoyed being there, and it was fun until a sergeant from another unit decided to let himself into my room in the middle of the night when I was sleeping and attempted to sexually assault me. It scared me so badly to wake up to that because of what had happened to me as a 14-year-old girl with my stepfather. My fight-or-flight response kicked in, and I ran like hell to another room on another floor of the barracks building where my friends were. They let me hide out and sleep on their couch for the rest of the night. Of course, I told them what had happened. I was so scared. They kept urging me to report the incident to the chain of command, but for whatever reason, I was afraid to. Fortunately for me, one of my friends that I had confided in went to my chain of command without my knowledge and informed them about what had happened.

This place was so different from my original duty station. Kriegsfeld, where I had endured levels of sexual harassment that today would have put the perpetrators in jail was a distant memory, up until that point. This duty station was a headquarters unit, so accountability was a huge deal; it was the first time I had actually seen someone held accountable for their actions. The man that assaulted me got an Article 15 (the military kiss of death) and lost his rank. He was knocked down to a private, and his wife left him and went back to the States. He stalked me all over the base. He would show up when I was out with my friends at the clubs or if we went to the mess hall for lunch or if we went to the track to run. It was the first time I had ever been stalked; it was creepy because he would just stand there, staring at me, never talking, just watching me.

Ultimately, I was sent back to Kriegsfeld since some of the soldiers I had a run-in with before had since returned to the States. I finished the final six months of my first tour in Germany there, and I have to say that was the longest six months of my entire life. The chain of command put me in a separate barracks apart from the other military police and assigned me to the administrative unit where I worked in the admin offices. They also alerted our gate security about the person stalking me because he had made multiple death threats via phone calls and notes that had been slid under my barracks door when I was still at the headquarters unit. For the first couple weeks that I was back at Kriegsfeld, I felt numb, like a ticking bomb. I had a small circle of friends that I did feel safe with: Arthur, Dustin, Larry, Tim, and Garth. They were a terrific bunch, and I was like their little sister. They took care of me like a band of brothers, and I finally felt like I was no longer prey.

The man that had been stalking me in the headquarters unit had somehow located me at Kriegsfeld and called me on the phone in my barracks building, on my floor. Thinking back, it still makes my skin crawl hearing his voice on the phone. He told me that he was going to kill me for ruining his career, and since headquarters was only about 90 minutes away, I was still accessible to him. When I finally did leave Kriegsfeld to come back to the US, I was never so happy to leave a place. The only thing in my life that could compare to it was leaving my mother's house when I first joined the army, but I'm not sure which one made me happier.

I came back to the US and was stationed on the East Coast when Iraq decided to invade Kuwait in 1990. I was deployed to the Persian Gulf in October of 1990 and spent a total of 187 days in the desert with only two showers. We were issued small stainless-steel bowls and six liters of non-potable water every day, which we could use to wash ourselves or our clothes. We were a mobile unit, living out of our vehicles and small tents, so we had no access to luxuries like running (or hot) water and flushing toilets.

We started our deployment near Riyadh, Saudi Arabia, and moved north from there. The further north we moved toward the Iraqi border, the food improved, from MREs to actual reconstituted meat, and of course, our pay went up as well because we were in imminent danger. Of course, there were no stores to spend in, so I was looking forward to having a good chunk of change saved up if I made it home. I had given my next-of-kin, my mother, power of attorney over my financial affairs while we were deployed so she could pay my car payments and other bills.

When I got back to the States from the deployment, our entire battalion received two weeks' leave. I was looking forward to packing up my car and taking a road trip to see my mom and the rest of the family back in Denver. Arriving stateside, I went to retrieve my car from the storage yard where we'd all stored our vehicles for the deployment and was informed that a company had tried to repossess it while it was sitting there. Since I had given my mother power of attorney over my finances to make my car payments, insurance, and all my other bills while I was gone, I assumed it was all taken care of. Back then, we were in the middle of nowhere in Saudi Arabia in 1990–91, and the internet had not yet been created. I had given my mom carte blanche over my finances to take care of my financial affairs while I was in the Gulf. I called my mom to find out what happened, and that's when she informed me that she and my stepdad had used every dime I had. They had cleaned me out completely. Every. Single. Penny.

It's no great wonder that I became very hard in my heart and very cold and indifferent to people, especially my family. But what's my point in sharing my story with you? I had an identity crisis my whole life. I had been thrown away, verbally scourged, and rejected. I was a two-time loser, confused about my purpose in life, if I even had one.

I had originally given my life to Christ when I was 17, after my parents went out and got religion, but I still struggled with who I was. I still had daddy issues, I still ran away, and I still made every mistake I could possibly make. I tried to tell God who I was, not the other way around. And although I was a Christian (it even said so on my dog tags,) I didn't follow Jesus; I ran as far as I could from Him instead.

All those years, I could have just turned to Him for the love and acceptance that I needed so badly, but in my foolhardiness, I believed I had to do life alone, that nobody else was going to be my superhero, that I wasn't significant enough, so I had to toughen up and do it for myself. And although not every person who reads this can relate on every level to my story, there are women out there who do relate to the sexual assaults, the bullying in their own home, or bearing their own scarlet letter and having an abortion in secret, like I did.

Do you ever feel like the enemy is trying to use your past against you too? I can tell you, friend, the enemy has tried in every stage of my life to keep me silenced. But God says in Jeremiah 1:5, "Before I formed you in the womb, I knew you; Before you were born, I sanctified you." This means that you and I have a few promises from God, that we not only have a purpose, an appointed calling over our lives, but also that He knew your name and mine before we even drew that first breath.

God planned and invested in your life before you were born. This means that you and I were born on purpose, with a purpose.

The enemy would have me believe that I am nothing, that my life has no meaning because of the lifelong struggle with my identity that began before I was born. My mother contemplated aborting me during her pregnancy and reminded me of it time and time again as I grew up, saying she should have followed through with it. My identity crisis began prior to my birth, and that was just the beginning.

I didn't know my dad and grew up with only a memory of him literally throwing me away. Add to that the sexual advances by my stepdad, and I was cemented in my lack of identity. It should come as no great surprise that I developed what we now call "daddy issues." Just like anybody else, I was looking for that approval and validation from my dad, and even from my step-dad, but I never received it.

Falling into my mother's pattern of teen pregnancy and dropping out of high school was me living in *her* mindset, repeating her mistakes. I was perpetuating the cycle or generational curse. The agonizing memories of my poor choices became fuel for the enemy to torment me with—guilt over being a high school drop-out and becoming a teen-pregnancy statistic resulting in abortion. My parents went out one day and got religion and proceeded to force-feed me with their newfound faith. I viewed my parents as hypocrites and wanted nothing to do with their God. They managed to get me to church a few times, and I finally came around at 17 and gave my life to God, but I was so deeply rooted in rebellion, I had no interest in getting to know Him. I went through the motions, and I prayed the "sinner's prayer." Even though I became "born-again," I still had no solid understanding of what it meant.

By the time I went into the army, it was only a matter of time before I reached my wit's end. Sexual harassment in the army—from being forced to watch pornography to witnessing a gang rape and being silenced with the threat of being next—caused a ripple effect in my life and left me afraid for my own safety, forcing me to defend myself.

I faced multiple threats, enemies seen and unseen, in the Persian Gulf during Operations Desert Shield and Desert Storm, including numerous soldier-on-soldier sex assaults, poor leadership oversight, and surviving the bombings when the UN deadline passed. I slept with a Gerber LMF knife under my pillow for at least a solid decade.

Army doctors told me I was fine and that the insomnia I'd had every night since the war would gradually go away on its own. The night terrors, flashbacks, sleepwalking, and waking up in a rage would all fade with time. They had me believing that "time heals all wounds." I had convinced myself that sleeping with a knife under my pillow was normal.

Eventually, at the behest of my husband, I had to seek help. He told me in no uncertain terms that he would be forced to divorce me if I didn't get help. It's unfortunate that his threat of leaving me was the catalyst that moved me into the VA healthcare system, but my sweet husband's ultimatum was the wake-up call I needed. When I finally did enroll for health care with the VA, I came away with the diagnosis that nobody, no soldier, no police officer ever wants to hear; I had post-traumatic stress disorder (PTSD). Although I still have some struggles, I will say that the PTSD counselors have helped me work through nearly five decades of rage, physical pain, and insomnia, and I am happy to report that I no longer sleep with a knife under my pillow.

What afflicted me most wasn't just the byproducts from the patterns of abuse I had endured in my childhood and in the army but also the lasting effects of self-loathing—never believing I was good enough, always believing that I was beyond help, that only pills could ease the pain. My self-hatred became more apparent through self-destructive behavior like smoking, drinking, bad relationship after bad relationship, taking extravagant risks that could easily cause me bodily harm or even death, a mouth that would make a sailor blush, and a desire to end my life as a means of escape from the pain of the memories. Mind you, I was a "Christian" through all these years. Reliving traumatic events whenever a "trigger" would present itself, I was a mess. I was saved but so very far away from the freedom that Christ provides for us.

Not only was I abused, but then I also gave those tormenting memories my permission to reignite anytime, anywhere, because I didn't realize I had a choice. The resulting anchors that formed in my life were anger, bitterness, unforgiveness, depression, and at one point, suicidal thoughts. Where most people would turn to alcohol, drugs, gambling, sex, or other similar vices to cope with their issues, I turned to anger and rage. Anger became my fuel—my addiction, if I'm honest—and I lived like that for most of my life. The rage would spring up at the stupidest moments over seemingly common and small issues like dropping something or seeing something that triggered a memory, certain noises, or even ambient light in a dark room while I was trying to sleep. My life was a huge eggshell, cracked and broken into a pulp, out of control, and irreparable.

The journey back from the land of the walking-wounded has probably been more difficult than going through the actual events that put me there. The good news is that Jesus came after me. Time and time again, there were invitations to go to church or Bible study and eventually I went. Thank God that He comes after us—I would have been lost long ago if He hadn't. I found a way back to life, a path through those dark places, and I know you will find a way back too.

If you hide emotional scars and wounds from past hurts, you are not alone. Satan wants you to believe you are alone because you are easier to manipulate if you go solo. His goal is to keep you small and silent. But you are not alone. Christ is with you. There is hope, an expectation of beauty in exchange for the ashes.

My poor decisions put me so far away from God that I never dared darken the doorway of any church, even though I was already saved. I was set free when God forgave my sins when I was 17. But I still chose to live in the guilt, shame, pain, and despair of my past, *and* I kept living as though I had no Savior or freedom in Christ. God's forgiveness was visible in me only when I finally stopped running away and came clean with God. I finally accepted the fact that I had sinned against Him. I rededicated my life to Christ Jesus as my Lord and Savior, in sincerity and truth, when I was 30 years old.

Getting real with God is a lifelong process about making peace with your past. When I finally got real with God about my pain, that is the exact crossroad where He helped me forgive those who hurt me, including myself, and I experienced life free of condemnation. God freed me from that internal prison of guilt, self-hate, and self-sabotaging thoughts—all behaviors that isolate you and me from our friends, family, and more importantly, from God. I know He wants to free you from that same prison too.

I can tell you that because of the love of the Father and the forgiveness of Jesus, I am a new creation in Christ, and although forgiving those who hurt me was a difficult and painful process, in the end, I found a freedom that surpasses all the hurt and disappointment. I still have good and bad days like anyone else. The difference in my day-to-day flow can be pinpointed to a few key elements of wisdom that I will share with you throughout this book. While terrible things have happened to me, things the enemy intended for my harm, God intended them for His glory and for my good.

Just because the enemy says something to you or about you does not make it true, yet millions of people, including our youth, allow the enemy to speak lies to us and about us every day. When we believe those lies of the enemy, we are making an agreement with him. Just spend five minutes watching the news or checking out social media, and you will witness the demise of someone. Friend, remember this: the moment you received Jesus as your Savior and gave your life to Christ, you became His. You are covered by His umbrella in the storm of life. Your identity is no longer you vs. the world. Jesus is your Champion, and when you decide to come clean with Him, your identity is made crystal clear. You are a member of His family, and He will defend His family to the very end. Just like an adoption that happens when a child is given a new identity in their adoptive family, you have been adopted into a family that resides under the wings of our Creator. You and I have an identity that can never be taken away, an all-access pass to healing, forgiveness, and restored relationships.

You will make mistakes along the way; we all do. The apostle Paul shared with us God's response to removing our "thorn," our imperfections, in 2 Corinthians 12:9. God said, "...that My grace is sufficient for you." It's okay to be imperfect because, guess what? News flash: you are imperfect. Perfection is a lie and something you and I will never reach. Salvation in Christ doesn't mean you or I *can become* perfect; on the contrary, it means we are made *righteous* in the presence of our Holy God *through* Christ Jesus alone. It is in His death on the cross and resurrection from the grave that the miracle happens. Jesus is the Lamb of God, who covers our sins with His precious blood. When you professed with your mouth and believed in your heart in Christ, His death, and resurrection, your identity in the world died and you received a brand new identity *in* Him. Honor what Jesus did on the cross for you by giving yourself permission to be imperfect.

What does this mean? Imagine your driver's license for a second. What state do you live in? If you were to move to a different state, then your driver's license would be reissued with the new state. Same picture, same person, hopefully the same height and weight, eye and hair color, but you would be a resident of that new state. That's how salvation works. Your state prior to Christ Jesus saving you is in the world. When you accept Christ Jesus as your Lord and Savior, you get a new ID card in a new state. Although the picture still looks like you, and height, weight, eye color, and hair color may stay the same, 2 Corinthians 5:17 says that the spirit inside you is made new. Your new driver's license is under the state of "saved by the blood of Jesus Christ." While salvation won't change the historical facts of your life or my life, it paves the way for you and me to live in victory despite the setbacks, the disappointments, and the bad decisions. You've been grafted into His family, and when you face the problems and storms of the world, you have a mighty Protector, Jesus, who will be on your side, fighting for you.

Let's take a quick inventory of how a mistaken identity might be affecting you in a negative way right now.

- Can you think of events in your own life when you have experienced hurt that left you internally scarred?

- As a believer in Christ Jesus, how much power do those incidents have over you today?

- Do you still find yourself sabotaging new relationships or going back to the thing that keeps you feeling guilty, like emotional eating or drinking?

- Do you find every muscle tightening when you think about particularly hurtful or traumatic events that occurred in your past?

- Do you relive the pain again and again? What does it feel like physically when you think about that event(s)?

You don't have to live with that pain. The enemy wants you to think that you are all alone and that there is no healing that will make you good enough or clean enough, no way that God can heal you or even love you. The enemy wants you to believe that God has left you. But let me tell you—not only is God ready, willing, and able to help you, He hasn't gone anywhere. He has been fighting for you from the moment you called for help.

As a single mother, when my daughter was just seven years old, my stepfather told me that God had left me. That I was beyond His blessing and would never be redeemed because I didn't deserve it. He was right on one count. I didn't deserve the healing God gave me, but God healed me anyway. I had a broken heart, and God put it back together. It didn't happen overnight, but it did happen. And He has your healing ready for you too.

If you are not saved, not a born-again believer in Christ Jesus and want to know more, I'd like to invite you to my website and blog, where I explore what it means to be saved and why you and I need it. Just go to gettingrealwithGod.com.

If you are ready to ask for God's help and forgiveness, the prayer below is my go-to:

Dear Father in heaven, I come to you broken, lost, lonely, and hurting. Father, please forgive me of my sins. I repent of my sins and choose Jesus. Lord, I believe that Jesus died for my sins on the cross, was laid in a tomb, and on the third day was resurrected from the dead. I ask You, Jesus, please come into my heart, and heal me, Lord. I ask You to be my Savior. Thank you for Your forgiveness and for your free gift of Salvation.

In Jesus' name, Amen.

2

WHO IS YOUR ENEMY?

How many legs does a dog have if you call his tail a leg?
Four. Saying a tail is a leg doesn't make it a leg.

—Abraham Lincoln

TO EVERY HERO, IT SEEMS THAT THERE IS AN ARCH-NEME-
sis, a behind-the-scenes mastermind with some sort of evil plan
to take over the world. To light, there is the dark. To Batman,
there is Joker. To Superman, there is Lex Luthor. And to Jesus,
there is Satan.

The Bible refers to Satan, the devil, or the enemy many times
throughout. In the book of Job, 1:6–7, we are told that the sons of
God came to present themselves to Him and that Satan was
among them. In verse 7, the Lord asks Satan where he came from,
and Satan's response is "from going to and fro on the earth, and
from walking back and forth on it." Friend, this means that we
coexist with our enemy, whether we want to or not. But just because we share common ground doesn't mean we have to lie
down and be Satan's next victim. Instead, the Bible tells us to be
sober and vigilant in 1 Peter 5:8 because "the devil walks about
like a roaring lion, seeking whom he may devour."

Specifically, Jesus said that we would have "tribulation" in the world (John 16:33) but to be of good cheer because He has overcome the world.

Satan and his servants live in the same world that you and I live in. His servants, or demons, prey upon people, as they have done since Adam and Eve. Satan is old and well-practiced in his trickery and deceit. But if the enemy lives in the world with us, is there a safe place you and I can live where Satan can't touch us? How do we protect ourselves, our homes, and our children from an enemy we can't even see? Where does that leave you and me, who belong to Christ Jesus?

In the military, soldiers learn early on in their careers that their primary purpose is to be part of something greater, and with that greater responsibility come great enemies. And what's more, each soldier must be trained to identify their enemy to keep the upper hand in case of an attack. Police officers are trained with that same mindset: how to spot a suspect with very little information and be prepared to protect life based on that information. The problem is that the threat can change so rapidly that it can become difficult to identify once chaos enters the scene. Police officers and soldiers alike (and yes, I can speak from experience on both counts) must assess on a continual basis how the threat is evolving around them. How is this accomplished? Training. Plain and simple, training and rote exercises are critical to successfully spotting dangers around you too.

So now you know you have an enemy, but how do you identify evidence of the enemy's presence in your life? After all, you can't see the enemy any more than you can see God, right? Well, faith works in both directions.

Remember, you have a purpose for your life, but your enemy has a purpose for your life too. First, let me say the enemy has had over 2,000 years of practice with targeting and bringing down the children of God. So if you think you can take him on by yourself, think again. John 10:10 says Jesus identifies the enemy as a thief, "the thief does not come except to steal, and to kill, and to destroy. I have come that they may have life and that they may have it more abundantly." It is significant that Jesus not only calls the enemy a thief, but He also gives the thief a distinct job description: to steal, to kill, and to destroy. Not one or the other, but all three are the enemy's purpose. And if the enemy is committed to his *why* (your destruction), you need to be doubly committed to your *why* as well: your identity, your life, and your God-anointed purpose in Christ Jesus. That is the reason Peter told us in 1 Peter 3:15 to "…always be ready to give a defense to everyone who asks you a reason for the hope that is in you."

Understanding your why is so important that without it, you can easily lose sight of what you are protecting: yourself and your family.

The enemy has an arsenal of weapons at his disposal. Yes, he has the go-to tools—ones that most of us have been exposed to at one time or another, like the feeling of guilt for something we did or did not do. For a decision gone wrong or even eating something we know we should not or indulging in something we knew we should have left alone. Those are classic examples of how the enemy steals our joy, our peace, our blessings, and even our calm. But what I want to share with you is the practical application or the tactics that the enemy is using against you to fulfill his purpose right now. In a nutshell, your enemy uses anything he can that puts a wall between you and God. The further you drift away from God, the more vulnerable you become, making it even easier for Satan to conquer you.

Jesus called Satan a *thief*, but in what way is he a thief? Say, for example, the door lock gets broken on your car. Then you would be forced to leave it open and unsecured all the time—but would you be comfortable doing this? I know I wouldn't. So you and I would do whatever it took to get the lock fixed and keep our car safe from thieves. Your mind is like that car, and if the lock is broken or even absent, the thief can come and go all day long. But he doesn't stop there.

The enemy also comes to *kill...* your dreams, your relationships, your hope, and you, if possible. His goal is to ultimately destroy you from the inside out. The enemy intentionally works to destroy you, your life, your family, and your career. To make matters even worse, he is laser-focused and an expert in his field, while you and I are novices, rookies if you will. But we are not fighting alone; Christ Jesus is in our corner, helping us.

Now that you know what the enemy wants to do, let's explore some of the ways he works to get what he wants.

The enemy is here to *steal*. What is he stealing though? Is it bigger than a breadbox? Is it something we can go buy and replace, or will insurance cover the loss of what was stolen? In reality, the thing the enemy wants is to steal *your relationship with God* by any means possible.

Hmm, how can one steal a relationship? Ask anyone who has been on either side of an unfaithful partner or spouse. Unfortunately, unfaithfulness happens because the enemy stole, or romanced away, the relationship. But *how* did he steal it? 1 John 2:16 says that "for all that is in the world—the lust of the flesh, the lust of the eyes, and the pride of life—is not of the Father but of the world." Going back to the car analogy, our own lust for attention, acceptance, validation, and love are areas where we have left our "cars unlocked."

Additionally, the enemy's goal is to *destroy...*everything about you and your life, your children, and their children. Total annihilation of God's most precious treasures, that is what Satan wants.

Paul wrote in Galatians 5:19 that "the works of the flesh are evident, which are: adultery, fornication, uncleanness, lewdness, idolatry, sorcery, hatred, contentions, jealousies, outbursts or wrath, selfish ambitions, dissensions, heresies, envy, murders, drunkenness, revelries and the like; of which I tell you beforehand, just as I also told you in the past, that those who practice such things will not inherit the kingdom of God." I can say with all conviction that I, along with everybody else, am guilty as charged. I have committed horrendous acts, and I have thought hateful, judgmental thoughts against others and against myself. I have worn slutty clothes for the purpose of seeking validation. I have been promiscuous. I have been falling-down drunk, smoked, tried drugs, and even had suicidal thoughts at different points in my life. It is true: if you and I have a pulse, then you and I have, in some way, sinned against God. Maybe we do not all use the same vices, but we follow what we want, what we *choose* to pursue, over God. It is not enough that at some point in our lives we took part in these types of activities or that we are still willing participants. The enemy, the accuser of the saints, uses our skeletons, our memories and feelings, our emotions and decisions, and our very humanity against us. But how does Satan do this?

Matthew 4:1–11 says that Jesus was led into the wilderness to be tempted by the devil. I believe that when this happened, Jesus gave us some critical clues, some intel as to how the enemy operates and what tactics he uses to try to bring us low. Satan attempted to gain access to Jesus' mind by appealing to His humanity, His pride, and His ego... all the things that you and I fall prey to today, yet Jesus was able to successfully escape the temptations that the devil put against Him. 1 Corinthians 10:13 says that "no temptation has overtaken you except such as is common to man; but God is faithful, who will not allow you to be tempted beyond what you are able, but with the temptation will also make the way of escape, that you may be able to bear it." God is aware of the temptations the enemy throws at you, but Jesus' example in the wilderness is a good example of how you and I should deal with it too.

> The problem is not that we do not have access to God's Word. Rather, we lack understanding of this critical dynamic because we don't invest time in reading it, and Satan knows this.

Jesus demonstrated what our actions should be when we are tempted by the devil. You see, Jesus answered each temptation with the Word of God. Literally. He didn't argue with the devil; He did not mince words or try to defend Himself. He did not try to solve the devil's problems, and He did not try to understand why the devil would try to tempt Him. Jesus did not run scared, and He did not back down. His response was quite simple. He responded with scripture, God's Word, which is where we, too, should be going for our own strength.

You and I tend to get it wrong when we overthink the temptation we are faced with. We want both the control *and* the credit for overcoming it. While this plays to the human ego, it also allows our pride to take over; our emotions and how we feel are all that matter, and in the end, that's all the enemy needs to get a foothold in your heart. Remember, the enemy hates you, so know up front that any temptation he throws at you is always for his benefit and not for yours.

Jesus warned us that the enemy is here to kill. Kill Him, you, and me. How many people have been driven into depression and suicide or commit homicide? A significant number on both accounts—just look at the suicide hotlines and calls for help from people who see no other way out of the depression that the enemy has them trapped in, or look at the news in any city where violent crime is on the rise, with shootings and stabbings increasing in number every day. Consider not just the number of suicides that occur every year but also the suicide attempts, the cutters, the drinkers, or those who die from drug overdoses.

But it doesn't stop there. How many times a week does your local news report on car crashes, home invasions, road rage incidents, domestic violence, and assaults that all result in death? The enemy came to kill and will continue in his purpose; you and I can't control what the enemy does. But never forget that James 5:16 says that "the effective, fervent prayer of a righteous man avails much." You and I, us believers in Christ Jesus, are key in helping not just ourselves in prayer but others as well. The apostle Paul reminds us in 1 Thessalonians 5:16–18 to "rejoice always, pray without ceasing, in everything give thanks; for this is the will of God in Christ Jesus for you."

While we share the human experience with non-believers, you and I made the conscious choice to draw our strength and protection from Christ Jesus the moment we accepted Him as our Lord and Savior, and it is our responsibility to "pray without ceasing." Paul further emphasizes in 1 Thessalonians 5:21–22 that we are to "test all things, hold fast what is good. Abstain from every form of evil." In this charge from Paul, you and I can be encouraged that by staying close to Jesus, we have authority over our homes, property, family, and community. Prayer is low-calorie, low-intensity and will help deepen your connection with God. It also helps God use you in your prayer life to lift up our families, neighbors and communities that are being ravaged by the evil one. Take action in your corner of the world, and pray without ceasing!

And let's not forget that the enemy also came to destroy. Let that saturate for a minute. Satan's third purpose is to destroy, but what can he destroy? Your heart, your mind, your family, your home, your career, your bank account, your health, your children's health... the list goes on and on. How does the enemy destroy these things in our lives? Consider for a minute the number of cancer, heart disease, or diabetes patients on any given day and tell yourself, "Test all things." Or examine the number of deaths caused by addictions to alcohol, pharmaceutical and illicit drugs, violence in our neighborhoods, and even criminal behavior. These are all orchestrated attacks by the enemy; his endgame is to destroy everything that God created.

The good news is that God is still in control, and although there are times when the enemy has successfully brought you and me low, Jesus is here to bring you back up. There are blessings for you despite the sickness and disease. Jeremiah 29:11 says, "For I know the thoughts that I think toward you, says the Lord, thoughts of peace and not of evil, to give you a future and a hope." Even when the enemy comes against you, God still intends your circumstance, your situation, to be for *your* good and His glory.

You see, when you and I were born-again, we went straight to the top of the devil's most-wanted list. The enemy does not want you to succeed, triumph, or have joy, even though the healing and blessings God has for you are already there for your receiving. Following Christ's example in the wilderness—speaking the Word of God to the temptation—may not feel like you are fighting or doing battle, but that's exactly what it is: a battle… for your mind. You don't have to let the enemy in the door just because he knocks on it.

I remember a time in my life as a single mom when the devil was wreaking havoc on my finances. Maybe you're a little short with money right now like I was, and the bills are due. It is easy enough to justify not tithing. I mean, the bills still have to be paid, right? But do not be tempted to skip your tithe. When you do, you unwittingly come into agreement with the enemy, which will prevent the abundance of God's blessing over your finances. This is an area that God dealt with me about years ago.

I fell into financial difficulties as a single mom, and at one point, I had to turn to the county for help. During this period of my life, I was looking for a job, as I had been out of work for a while. I also didn't have transportation because my car had been repossessed. I had $67 to my name. As I said, God had been speaking into my spirit about my tithe, and He was trying to lead me to where I could trust Him fully. I remember being so scared of letting go of that $67 because it was all I had left, and I still had bills due, groceries to buy, and my daughter to take care of.

That Sunday I went to church, and during the worship service, I was still trying to plead with God about my need to keep the money. God told me, "Test Me in this." When the collection plate came my way, I tithed all of it; it quite literally was every single penny that I had. Strangely enough, though, I felt so much peace settle over me.

The next morning my pastor called me. I was at my dining room table reading my Bible, and my daughter was at school. Pastor Vince said, "Annamarie, I need to ask you if you still need a car."

"Yes," I replied.

"Well, I must tell you what happened this morning. A member of the church brought a car over to the church garage and told them that he was donating that car to a single mother in need. Is there any way that you can come over to the garage tomorrow to pick it up? We're going to have the maintenance team go through it today, and we are going to put new tires on it and change all the fluids before you take it."

As I write this and remember that phone call with Pastor Vince, my mind is still blown, and I am still in awe at how good God is. When God told me to test Him with my tithe, I never expected a car. Sure, I needed one, desperately, because I needed to find a job and get my daughter back and forth to school. He knew my need, and He not only had the blessing ready for me to receive it, He wanted to bless me, but my desire to keep that small amount of money was preventing me from receiving my miracle. My mind was fixed on the small, when God wanted me to fix my eyes on Him instead. The solution was already there, waiting for God to release it. Until I was ready to be obedient to what God was asking of me, the blessing was withheld. You see, God wants to bless us, but our disobedience ties His hands.

When I finally decided to yield to God and tithe, I held nothing back—not one penny. All the while, God had my blessing ready to give to me, and in my obedience, God was able to release the blessing into my life. The church not only had the car running and ready, but they signed the title over to me, so it was not just a loaner car—I *owned* the car free and clear. That's how good, how complete, our God is. That car gave me the ability to find a job with dependable transportation, provide for my daughter, and get her to school and home every day.

Truly, all things are possible in Christ, and God blessed me so much that day. But I don't want you to miss the critical key in my sharing this story with you. God had been dealing with me regarding my tithing for some time. I kept telling Him that I couldn't afford to tithe because I needed money to pay this bill or that bill or buy groceries... on and on. I gave every excuse I had, but all along, He kept telling me to test Him in this. I kept justifying my disobedience to God, but he is not interested in hearing our excuses. He is interested in our obedience to do what He is asking us to do. When you're a single mother living on table scraps with no vehicle, no job, and barely enough child support to keep your child in school, you don't get to have a lot of options. I felt that I was a better judge of how I needed to spend my money than God, which makes me laugh now when I think about how immature my attitude was, when I would respond to God with "but I need this money for..."

When thoughts creep in that put you against God, especially thoughts that keep justifying disobedience, remember what Christ Jesus said in John 10:10: "The thief (Satan) does not come except to steal, and to kill, and to destroy. I have come that they may have life and that they may have it more abundantly." He didn't come so that you and I could live like a sickly doormat; that is the lie of the enemy. Measure those thoughts against what the Bible says, bring them into your prayer life, and ask God what He is trying to show you.

The enemy is after your wallet as well, and if you let him, the devil will take control of that too. We are stewards over our finances, and overspending—taking on more than you can actually handle—is another way we come into agreement with the enemy.

God blesses us with things like solid careers, an income, and the ability to provide for our families, put a roof over our heads, and food on the table. God cares about the little things like keeping the lights on, the water running, and making sure that the trash gets picked up every week. Realize the enemy uses all those small details that make up your existence to bring about destruction in your household; essentially, they can become idols. When you and I overspend or obsess over the things that are on the wants-not-needs list, we take God off the throne in our mind and instead focus on the thing that we want but do not actually need. When you cave to this type of temptation, rest assured the enemy is right there, stroking your ego and puffing up your pride. When you come back to reality, which usually happens when the credit cards come due, the sticker shock/obligation leaves you suspended in anxiety.

What am I saying? Remember 1 Thessalonians 5:21? It says, "Test all things; hold fast what is good." Here is a simple exercise to help you test all things in your life. You do have an abundance in your life right now, and if for any reason you're not convinced that you do, then try this.

Take a plain piece of paper and draw a line down the middle. On the left side, list all the things that you don't have but want, and on the right side, list all the things that you do have but do not necessarily need. Does anything jump off the page at you? Circle it. The circled items identify the areas in your life where the enemy has tried (or succeeded) to tempt you or lead you away from God. These are the items that you need to bring to God in prayer. These "keys" identify what items in your life the enemy is using against you. This is a strategic operation— exposing how the enemy goes to work for your destruction.

The enemy's toolbox contains weapons that you and I don't understand, but the Bible tells us in Ecclesiastes 1:9 that "there is nothing new under the sun." The decisions you and I make are not a surprise to God. Romans 5:8 says that "God demonstrates His own love toward us, in that while we were still sinners, Christ died for us." Even while you and I were still *choosing* to be led away by those things you listed in the exercise above, continuing to live in our sin, Jesus was diligent and obedient to the cross, to His death, and ultimately His resurrection. He did that so you and I would have life in victory in Him, to have a fighting chance against sin and death. Don't just take my word for it; test Him in this!

3

SWIMMING UPSTREAM

Perpetual optimism is a force multiplier.

—Colin Powell

WE HAVE TALKED ABOUT WHO YOU ARE AND WHO YOUR enemy is, but do either of these topics have any impact on how the world, everyone around you, will perceive you as a child of the Most High God? Know that from the moment you accepted Jesus Christ as your Lord and Savior, you became a target of the enemy. Satan hated you before you trusted in Jesus, and when you became a born-again believer, you went straight to the top of Satan's ten most-wanted hit list. People who are not saved are not going to understand your source of joy and happiness, and that's ok. The world will have issues with you just because you are a Christian, making it more important than ever to spend time with God every day. Jesus told us in John 15:18–19, "If the world hates you, you know that it hated Me before it hated you. If you were of the world, the world would love its own. Yet because you are not of the world, but I chose you out of the world, therefore the world hates you." It's not a question of "if" the world will hate you, but more a question of when and to what degree of intensity.

Remember that our enemy came to steal, to kill, and to destroy you, me, our families, our jobs, our finances, our children, our property—everything directly related to you and me is the enemy's target. We also acknowledge that the world does not necessarily believe in or share our hope in our Lord, Christ Jesus. In fact, many people will challenge your beliefs, some out of their own ignorance, some out of their own petulance, and some out of their own rebellion. Stay in the Word every single day and it will strengthen and fortify you. 1 Peter 3:15 tells us to "always be ready to give a defense to everyone who asks you a reason for the hope that is in you, with meekness and fear." Whether you were saved this morning or 50 years ago, challenges, questions, and curiosity about your relationship with Christ Jesus will come up in the most surprising of situations.

There will be days when it's going to feel like you are going against the flow—dead set against the status quo. The news outlets will tell you to be afraid of some new disease and that you should hide in your house until the government tells you to come out. But that kind of irrational fear does not affect you and me because our hope is in the Lord; rather, the joy in having an active relationship with Christ Jesus strengthens you and me through life in spite of what *they* tell you to be afraid of because we as believers draw our strength from Living Waters.

In John 4:1–18, Jesus meets a woman at a well in Samaria. She is average, at least by the world's standards. She had been promiscuous, sleeping around town, multiple marriages under her belt. How many of us women can relate to that? John tells us that in the sixth hour of the day, she chooses to go to the well. What's interesting here is that she went to the well when she knew nobody else would be there. Essentially, she was hiding from the judging eyes of the people in the city because of her promiscuity and shame. Her conversation with Jesus reveals something so important to you and me that I don't want you to miss it.

A woman of Samaria came to draw water from a well where Jesus was sitting. He said to her, "Give me a drink."

"How is it that You, being a Jew, ask a drink from me, a Samaritan woman?"

"If you knew the gift of God, and who it is who says to you, 'Give Me a drink,' you would have asked Him, and He would have given you living water," Jesus replied.

"Sir, You have nothing to draw with, and the well is deep. Where then do You get that living water? Are You greater than our father Jacob, who gave us the well and drank from it himself, as well as his sons and his livestock?" the woman asked.

Jesus responded, "Whoever drinks of this water will thirst again, but whoever drinks of the water that I shall give him will never thirst. But the water that I shall give him will become in him a fountain of water springing up into everlasting life."

This got her attention! "Sir, give me this water, that I may not thirst nor come here to draw," she said.

Jesus told her, "Go, call your husband, and come here."

"I have no husband," she replied.

Jesus said to her, "You have well said, 'I have no husband,' for you have had five husbands, and the one whom you now have is not your husband; in that, you spoke truly."

Jesus knew, before the conversation took place, what her circumstances—what her choices—had been and what her life looked like. And even though He knew of her lifestyle and choices, He still chose her. You and I are not unlike her; we have made bad decisions and lived with the consequences of our actions. The good news is that Jesus still chose you, and He still chose me, even while we were still sinning. He knew the dirty truth about her, about you, and about me, and He still chooses us and loves us anyway.

The world will not understand this relationship that we have with Jesus because we no longer allow the enemy to use our guilt and bad decisions against us. We don't need to hide our skeletons anymore—just like the woman at the well. He already knows your dirty, dark secrets, but when you and I come clean with Jesus, we are like a school of salmon, swimming upstream against the current of the rushing waters in the river of life. Being in a relationship with Christ Jesus is living in honesty and humility, and it can be a demanding journey; however, it's not an impossible one.

Jesus said in John 4:23–24 that "the hour is coming, and now is, when the true worshipers will worship the Father in spirit and truth; for the Father is seeking such to worship Him. God is Spirit, and those who worship Him must worship in spirit and truth."

It all comes down to where you find the source of your strength because that source is what carries you from day to day. I believe that Christ gave us an excellent example of where to draw our strength from in John 14:26. He said, "But the Helper, the Holy Spirit, whom the Father will send in My name, He will teach you all things and bring to your remembrance all things that I said to you." If you are a believer, the Helper is available whenever and wherever you need Him.

Asking God to give us strength when we are weak is not only scriptural but also a game changer. There will be times when a relationship might go sour, and that man you thought was "the one" walked out on you and broke your heart. Or maybe the people at work can't relate to you, and you feel like an outcast, never getting invited to lunch with the clique. Or you may encounter someone like me, for whom God didn't exist in the home growing up, mouth like a trucker, a few tattoos, and knee-deep in rebellion.

You've laid your life down for Christ's sake, and if you continue to grow in your relationship with Him, you will never be alone. When you and I were born-again, we died to the flesh, but there was no magic wand that changed your personality, your favorite color, your bad habits, your language, or even your thoughts. There is no "instant-perfection" recipe that automatically changes you as a person. The changes that do occur in you and me are on God's timeline. When I dedicated my life to Christ, I was still a smoker. I still used bad language, and I still got tattoos. It took a few years, but eventually, God removed my desire to smoke. Things that used to appeal to me no longer hold my interest. I am still a work in progress with the bad language, if I'm honest. I know cuss words, or my "thorn," will be removed from me, but even if it is never removed, God's grace is still sufficient for me, and I am still a child of the Most High God.

1 Corinthians 13:11 says, "When I was a child, I spoke as a child, I understood as a child, I thought as a child; but when I became a man, I put away childish things." As you and I continue to grow in our relationship with God, subtle changes will occur, and eventually we will feel the impact of that verse in our lives. Life before Jesus was childish, foolish even, but now you and I are growing up. But just because you mature doesn't mean that the world around you is growing *with you*. Friends that you have known your whole life will find they no longer have things in common with you, and you will also realize that you no longer have much in common with them. It's okay if they don't want to accompany you on this journey. Your job is to love them anyway and keep on keeping on with Jesus.

Swimming upstream is not always popular or fun; it can even get a little lonely at times. Satan will put in overtime if he thinks it will isolate you. When you are all alone, it is easier to keep you discouraged and much easier to attack you. You must choose to stay in the Word of God daily. Sometimes it can feel overwhelming, but you don't have to bear the burden alone. There are plenty of resources available to you, like my daily Dive Into Proverbs (DIP), which you can sign up to receive via email by going to gettingrealwithgod.com.

If you do not have a local church that you attend regularly, find a Bible-based one near you. It may seem like spending time with God can be cumbersome, but instead of looking at it from the "spending" perspective, look at it as an "investment" in your future. I promise that if you stay consistent in building your relationship with God, the foundation of your life as a believer will be stronger than you could ever imagine. If you have the time and the means, consider getting involved with your local church volunteering. There are always ministries that need extra hands like yours. Just get involved and see where God takes you.

You will always have the majority with God on your side, even when people make fun of you, laugh at you for being square, or do not include you because they think you are a goody-two-shoes because you're a Christian. You plus God equals the majority. Remember, these people will not judge you in that holy appointment in the sky; God will.

2 Corinthians 4:2–4 says we have "renounced the hidden things of shame, not walking in craftiness or handling the Word of God deceitfully." It goes on to say, "but if our gospel is veiled, it is veiled to those who are perishing, whose minds the god of this age has blinded, who do not believe, lest the light of the gospel of the glory of Christ, who is the image of God should shine on them." This means that people who do not know Christ as their Lord and Savior are blind to the truth that you and I have found in Jesus. It also means that we should turn away from doing things that cause us to be in shame and not misuse our convictions in the Bible or in Jesus, not judging people, but instead, just love them. If they ask questions, speak boldly about what you believe because who knows who might be listening to you and whose life might be saved just by hearing the truth come from *you*.

Matthew 5:10–12 says, "Blessed are those who are persecuted for righteousness's sake, for theirs is the kingdom of heaven. Blessed are you when they revile and persecute you and say all kinds of evil against you falsely for My sake. Rejoice and be exceedingly glad, for great is our reward in heaven, for so they persecuted the prophets who were before you." Rest easy when the enemy throws you curve balls. God knows what you need before you even have the problem, the dilemma, or the decision. Turn to Him in prayer for answers. God never promises that life will be "easy street" when you choose Him, but He does promise to be with you through every storm.

Remember:

1. When you and I were saved, it did not mean that our human nature became perfect and we would suddenly act accordingly. On the contrary, we will never be perfect in and of our own selves or of our own efforts. The nice thing is that we are not told to go out and be perfect in the world. Instead, we are instructed to do two things in Matthew 22:37: "You shall love the Lord your God with all your heart, with all your soul, and with all your mind...Second...you shall love your neighbor as yourself."

2. Our identity is confirmed under the name of Jesus from the moment we are born again. In John 3:1–21, there was a man named Nicodemus. He came by cover of night to ask Jesus a question. He came at night because he was "of the Pharisees"—ashamed to be seeking out Jesus since Nicodemus was a "teacher of Israel." Nicodemus did not want anybody to know he was there. Jesus is awesome—He called Nicodemus out right then and there.

   "We know that you are a teacher and that God is with you because nobody could do what you do unless God was with him," Nicodemus said.

   Jesus responded, "Let me just say that unless you are born again, you cannot enter into the kingdom of God."

"Ummm, how does that work? A grown man cannot be born when he is old! How can he? Does he go back into his mother's womb?" Nicodemus asked.

"You have to be born of water and of Spirit to enter the kingdom of God," Jesus explained. "And as Moses lifted up the serpent in the wilderness, even so must the Son of Man be lifted up, that whoever believes in Him should not perish but have eternal life. For God so loved the world that He gave His only begotten Son, that whoever believes in Him should not perish but have everlasting life. For God did not send His Son into the world to condemn the world, but that the world through Him might be saved. He who believes in Him is not condemned; but he who does not believe is condemned already, because he has not believed in the name of the only begotten Son of God."

3. We are His adopted children, with an inheritance and rights granted to us by the Blood of the Lamb. We are no longer on our own, trudging through life as a solo act. Like a bride taking her husband's name when she marries, she has a new identity and is covered under her husband's name. Similarly, we are covered, or protected, under the name of Jesus, and He takes this covering, or protecting, of you and me very seriously.

PART 2

TO HATE
ONE ANOTHER

4

WHY SHOULD I FORGIVE THEM?

Where the mind goes, the body follows.

—Bruce Lee

AS A MAN OR A WOMAN OF GOD, YOU HAVE HOPEFULLY had some exposure to Matthew 6:14–15, which says, "For if you forgive men their trespasses, your heavenly Father will also forgive you. But if you do not forgive men their trespasses, neither will your Father forgive your trespasses." Forgiveness is a cut-and-dry issue, but when it comes down to it, do you and I really have the will, the desire, to forgive somebody who's wronged us? What if the person we need to forgive is ourselves? I mean, if God forgave you but you don't forgive you, then how do you and I live in victory if we are constantly putting ourselves down?

We have all been through good and bad times. I've shared with you some of the deepest hurts in my life. Maybe you had a rough childhood like mine, maybe not.

Maybe you developed "daddy issues" like I did; maybe you have no clue what that means but still managed to walk a dangerous path in rebellion. Why is it so important to bring these things up? I mean, those events were in the past, right?

Every day when you go about your life, you will meet people who seem to have it all together and appear to be happy, living a great life, and having a lot of things you wish you had. But here's the thing… they, too, are dealing with broken hearts and broken dreams, disappointments, and struggles, just like you and me. We all need to be encouraged to forgive, but we lack the spiritual muscles to do so.

I was an innocent two-year-old child when my father attempted to kill me. I didn't ask to be thrown into a radiator, and I certainly didn't deserve it. I have asked the Lord time and time again, "Why did I survive that traumatic event when so many other children who fall victim to child abuse die from their injuries?" Years later, my dad expressed his sorrow for his actions and that he vented out of anger toward my mother. Basically, he hurt me as a means of hurting her.

I remember years later in Germany hearing about a fellow soldier in Germany who had murdered his two-year-old daughter. He picked her up and threw her into walls, furniture and the ceiling, again and again, breaking several bones in her body. The abuse ended when he threw her off the second-story balcony of their apartment. She survived it all but ultimately died choking on her own blood. So why was I spared and not her? That is a question I'll never have the answer to, but I can tell you that finding the power to forgive my dad, who had tried to kill me in the same manner, was rather difficult in my own strength. It was several years after I came clean with God about my anger and hatred toward my dad before I was ready to face my dad and forgive him.

It was interesting to discover that while God was working in me, He was also working in my dad.

My dad was a police officer for over two decades, and like the rest of us, he had his issues. For most people, when we do something that offends someone or even commit a criminal act, it is typically a private issue. My dad's sins were blasted all over the news when he stepped out on his second marriage with a minor. His career was ruined, his retirement forfeited, and he lost everything from his house, his wife, his family, his cars, and even the friends he'd made throughout his career. He also went to prison, which you can well imagine is not kind to anyone, and even less so when the prisoner was a police officer.

He had written to me asking that I visit him in prison; I was still in the army at the time and was stationed in Fort Carson. I remember reading his letter and rejecting it immediately. I had no interest in seeing him, and his writing to me made me feel even more angry. "Why should I go visit him? He never went out of his way for me or my brother. What makes him think he was so special that I should make a three-hour drive to Canon City to see him?" I still went to see him, growing angrier with every mile. After all, this is the man who tried to kill me, who never gave me the time of day growing up, had a second family, and never invited me or my brother to be part of it, and now he has shamed our entire family name due to his own bad decisions.

I should have been elated to see him in his ruin, coming into the visitor's area in his prison clothes, a washed-up has-been. But I realized that my dad was just a man, not unlike the men that I had jailed in my own career as a police officer. Dad had a sin nature just like everybody else, and laying eyes on him like that, I didn't feel anger. I felt confusion more than anything. I saw a man who had literally lost everything because of his bad decisions.

He thanked me for coming to visit him, told me how proud he was of me, and asked me to forgive him. Just like that. Twenty years after he tried to end my life, I'm supposed to just be all happy and forgiving? Nope, not me. I told him I forgave him, but deep down, I knew I was a liar. Not only did I not forgive him; I was even more angry that on top of nearly killing me and abandoning my brother and me, he also ruined our family name. I was confused about why he wanted my forgiveness when he had thrown me away as a baby, because my voice clearly didn't count. After years of struggling with trying to find my own identity, here was this man, my dad, whose moral obligation was to claim me as his child yet attempted to end my life when I was just a baby. This man was now asking for my forgiveness.

I left there confused, hurt, and angry, wondering why he cared so much for my forgiveness when he never cared for me to begin with. In my life before Jesus, I was bitter, cold, and unforgiving to those that wronged me, including my dad. And I remembered his offenses against me as though they had just happened that same day. I wanted judgment, not mercy. I wanted him to feel the hate in me against him as punishment for what he did to me. I cared nothing for him or for any person that hurt me at that point in my life. I was dead inside; the only fuel I knew was the hatred I had for people, especially men. All men, including my dad, including the soldiers from my first duty station and the war, including boyfriends—all of them. In my mind, there was nothing good or honorable in men. Nothing.

In the years that followed, I am happy to report that I did finally get to know my dad, and although it took a few years, I finally came clean with God about my feelings of anger and hatred for him, and I did forgive him. In my mid-thirties, after I had re-dedicated my life to Christ, he asked for my permission to be a part of my life. The first time we met in person, I was braced for disappointment, I admit, but I remained hopeful. I had been in prayer about my relationship with my dad for years and had asked God to restore that relationship. It was awkward at first, much like a blind date. Not wanting to ignore the obvious elephant in the room, we talked candidly about that day when he threw me into that radiator, an action he had always regretted and could never take back. I believe he was sorry when he apologized to me, and in truth, I did finally forgive him.

When I visited my dad in prison years ago and lied about forgiving him, I carried that around like a backpack full of rocks. Every time I thought about my lie, another invisible stone was added to the backpack, weighing me down. What I found in forgiving my dad was that the enemy wanted me to stay angry. You see, Satan uses anybody and everybody, any situation to manipulate and destroy us. I spent over 30 years hating this man, allowing the enemy to torment me again and again with the memories of what happened, replaying that day constantly. I allowed memories like this one to taint relationships with men, in dating, in my career, and in friendships, never feeling like I was worth loving. I would sabotage relationships and stay isolated in my anger because I was comfortable there. I was a victim, and I was content to live as a victim.

When I finally came clean with God about my anger toward my dad and asked for God's forgiveness for harboring the event, that became the turning point in my ability to forgive him. I had been using my victim card, keeping hold of my anger, justifying my rage. I finally admitted to my dad that I had lied about forgiving him and forgave him for real, in spirit and truth. That is how I came to understand what forgiveness really meant.

Just think—what if God forgave in the same way that we do? My dad had tried to end me, that was true, but he honestly attempted to reconcile with me. Not only had I refused, but I also lied to him about it and said I forgave him. When we come to ask for forgiveness from our Father in heaven, we expect Him to hold true to His promise to forgive our sins and forget the incident altogether. This is what unconditional love looks like. But you and I place conditions on the forgiveness. "I'll forgive you this time; just don't let it happen again." God never says that to us; instead, His forgiveness is complete and total and without condition. He doesn't give a timeline or keep a running tab on your behavior. What He gives is real forgiveness with no conditions, and it is our job to model that same type of forgiveness.

In Matthew 18:21–35, Jesus paints a vivid picture of the consequences of not forgiving one another. He talks about a king who wanted to settle accounts with his servants. And when he had begun to settle accounts with his servants, one was brought to him who owed him ten thousand talents. But as he was not able to pay, his master commanded that he be sold, with his wife and children and all that he had, and that payment be made. The servant therefore fell down before him, saying, 'Master, have patience with me, and I will pay you all.' Then the master of that servant was moved with compassion, released him, and forgave him the debt.

But that servant went out and found one of his fellow servants who owed him a hundred denarii; and he laid hands on him and took him by the throat saying, 'Pay me what you owe!' So his fellow servant fell down at his feet and begged him, saying, 'Have patience with me, and I will pay you all.' And he would not, but went and threw him into prison until he should pay the debt. So when his fellow servants saw what had been done, they were very grieved, and came and told their master all that had been done. Then his master, after he had called him, said to him, 'You wicked servant! I forgave you all that debt because you begged me. Should you not also have had compassion on your fellow servant, just as I had pity on you?' And his master was angry and delivered him to the torturers until he should pay all that was due to him.

So My heavenly Father also will do to you if each of you, from his heart, does not forgive his brother his trespasses. (Matt. 18:23-35)

It was a whole different perspective when it was me doing the forgiving. It makes me wonder how God feels when we finally get over ourselves and admit our wrongdoing and finally seek His forgiveness. The feeling of being restored to Him enriches the relationship so much the joy cannot be contained!

When my dad and I finally got to know each other, he turned out to be a terrific person—nothing how I remembered him. In his final years, we had a great friendship, filled with good memories of a man that I now know was proud of me. That horrible, abusive incident that I had carried my whole life had finally lost its power to hurt me.

Satan lost his influence in my life as far as relationships with men were concerned, and I don't mean just in a dating capacity. I mean any men: supervisors, superiors, coworkers, subordinates, classmates, you name it. I had no trust in men through my army career, through my first marriage, and even through my career as an IT nerd. Men had been a source of pain for me my whole life. Once I forgave my dad, I was able to forgive my stepdad, my ex-husband, and yes, even the soldiers in Germany.

Mark 11:25–26 says, "Whenever you stand praying, if you have anything against anyone, forgive him, that your Father in heaven may also forgive you your trespasses. But if you do not forgive, neither will your Father in heaven forgive your trespasses." Anytime you have something against someone, and it comes to your mind, be quick to forgive it. That is the directive to you and me. God is quite serious about this forgiveness business. It is important to allow this critical concept to absorb into your spirit. The sooner you learn the art of forgiving, the sooner you'll be able to kick the devil out on his rear and experience joy and freedom on a whole new level.

I believe that bitterness, unforgiveness, is a cancer to the soul. While you are justified in your anger, the longer you meditate on the hurt, the pain, the betrayal, you allow the enemy to keep his foot in the door to your heart, giving him a foothold that prevents you from living in the freedom that Christ died for. It's time to break free from the memories that profit you nothing. Yes, the hurt is real, but friend, God takes forgiveness seriously, and so should you.

5

WHAT COMES OUT OF A MAN'S OR WOMAN'S MOUTH

Reacting in anger or annoyance will not advance one's ability to persuade.

—Ruth Bader Ginsberg

I RECENTLY HAD A REALLY BAD DAY AT WORK. I HAVE BEEN there in my position for a considerable length of time and very rarely have a bad day. I am blessed in my work and do not want to complain or be whiny, so I refer to a bad day as a "character-building" day. I was tested in my patience, my virtue, my ability to keep my mouth shut, my language, and my body language, and I will admit, I really struggled with it. I wrestled with being polite in the face of being treated rudely. I struggled with being ordered to do something when I knew it was not the right thing for me to do at the time.

Sometimes it can be difficult to take the so-called "high road." But understanding who our enemy is and the tactics that he uses against us—like using someone else's rudeness to tempt us to be rude back, use bad language, or cuss somebody out—I could easily have lost my temper. But there's something foundationally wrong with answering anger and rudeness with anger and rudeness.

In Psalms 37, David wrote, "Rest in the Lord, and wait patiently for Him; do not fret because of him who prospers in his way, because of the man who brings wicked schemes to pass. Cease from anger and forsake wrath; do not fret—it only causes harm."

David twice says *do not fret*. Why? Because it only causes harm. But how does fretting or worrying cause harm? As a woman, isn't it part of our DNA to worry and fret about every little thing? Meditating on the worry—the problem, the mistreatment, the abuse, the bullying, the thing you disagree with, the thing that hurt you—produces anxiety in us. When we give way to fretting, we are allowing the hurt, angry feelings to sit on the throne in our minds and nurture our victim mentality. But God will not share the throne with anything.

In the moment when the problem occurs, you have a choice to make. Responding to something out of anger is a very normal human response; however, the Bible says to be angry but do not sin. When the worry, the anger, and the hate come sailing into our mind, we make a decision. We can choose to let it go, and move on, or we can put it on the throne in our mind and take God off that throne allowing the racy, spiteful, angry thoughts to stay, causing our focus to leave God. This is called "meditating" on thoughts and feelings. We can meditate on God's Word and let Him develop our spiritual muscles, or we can meditate on the hurt and the person that caused it, which is kind of like living off junk food for your soul.

Meditating on thoughts and feelings involves unseen things, like judgment, gossip, and even jealousy and hate. Eventually, you will back up those thoughts with actions. The action could be starting or engaging in an argument. It could be a physical fight or destructive behavior like throwing something across a room. It could even be road rage, driving your car aggressively in order "teach the other guy a lesson." Giving in to the thoughts and feelings that made you angry or hurt can cause you and me to act in an irrational way, purposely trying to get back at the person who hurt us.

The problem here is that when you respond to anger, hurt or disappointment with anger, from a place of pride/ego, it only propagates the cycle and hurts you more because of the time and emotional effort involved in "dwelling on it." You're the one who is stuck crying, shaking, and lashing out because nobody understands. You are also the one who is an easier target in this condition because when the enemy has you all alone and dwelling on the pain, you are much easier for him to manipulate.

By allowing these intangible things like hurt feelings and emotions to run amuck, you will quickly see the very tangible fallout that results. Proverbs 21:23 tells us that "whoever guards his mouth and tongue keeps his soul from troubles." The easiest way to guard your mouth and tongue is to stop fretting over things that you have zero control over. Instead, give it to God, which is far easier said than done. When we get ticked off, praying is the last thing we usually think of when it should be the first. Your actions will always follow your mind. You can choose to pray, or you can choose to dwell. Either choice will be accompanied by a consequence. Praying and giving it to God will give you peace and grace to get through the situation. Choosing to dwell on it will evoke feelings that reek of victimhood, and any actions that come from this mindset will have an ill effect. Remember this: do the things you can, and let God take of the things that you can't.

Take, for example, a coworker who just got a pay raise. They do less work than you do, show up late every day, gossip about everybody, are never prepared for any meetings, and take two-hour lunches. You think you should be the one to get the pay raise; after all, you're on time every day, always prepared for meetings, and you always finish assigned projects on time, even staying late sometimes just to make sure that the work is complete. If you choose to complain, gossip about them to other coworkers, or become passive-aggressive by avoiding them any time they are around you, there will be consequences, even if you are justified in the complaint.

Gossiping about them, grumbling, or harboring offended feelings will make it more difficult for you to enjoy your job. Complaining and dwelling on the negative can be turned into a tool that the enemy uses to steal your peace and joy. While you may have a good case against the coworker, God still says to be patient and wait on Him. You don't know the details of that person's situation, but judging them or complaining about them will only count against you. Every moment you spend complaining is one less moment God could be pouring a blessing over your head. Every bitter thought and feeling you place on the throne of your mind places distance between you and God because He will not share the throne with anything.

You must choose Him over the hurt, over the bad break, over the abuse, over the assault, over the stolen items, over the foreclosure, and over the disappointment. When you call the thought, the event, or the hurt feelings captive and ask God to take over, you remove it from the throne of your mind. When you and I yield to God in this way, we keep Him on the throne of our minds, and He will fight the battle for us. All we need to do is keep our minds fixed on Him—fixed on Jesus.

The last thing to remember here is that the enemy is always listening to you. Not so much because you have such a dazzling personality and the whole world hinges on the edge of their seats, waiting to hear what you have to say... no, the enemy is taking notes because he plans to use whatever you say against you later. Gossiping and backbiting are activities that grieve the Holy Spirit for several reasons.

Gossip and backbiting go together, as they are outward spoken words against or about something that we are judging. It could be about someone's clothes, possessions, hair style, teeth, height, house, car, manicure, marital status, age, gender, job, education, or any variable about them. It could also be how long they took for lunch, whether they got to the office before or after you, or anything that is below the standard you have set for them.

The problems arise when they don't meet our standards — which will never happen. They not only don't know your standards, but they also don't care because they are busy worrying about their own lives. We begin to compare ourselves to them, putting ourselves on a pedestal as if we were better than they are. This is also the enemy appealing to your pride and ego. You and I can say, "Hey everybody, look at how good I am!" This is not a response that God will back you on.

Ephesians 2:8–9 says, "For by grace you have been saved through faith, and that not of yourselves; it is the gift of God, not of works, lest anyone should boast." No matter how good we might think we are, Jesus leveled the playing field. When you are tempted to lift yourself up by comparing the actions of others to yourself, remember what Paul told us in Romans 3:23, that "all have sinned and fall short of the glory of God."

When you or I pass judgment on someone, we are putting ourselves on a pedestal when we people are all equal in God's eyes. The moment you gave your life to Christ and accepted His forgiveness, you also accepted the responsibility not just to love God but also to love your neighbor. It is difficult to love and honor something when you are talking badly about it.

I knew a woman who was not particularly happy in her marriage, her third marriage, in fact. We were out at a restaurant having dinner, along with several other couples. At one point, her husband left the table to use the restroom, and she immediately began talking about him in a very unfavorable way. How he does not do enough, does not meet her expectations, does not take care of the kids often enough, and on and on. We were all quite embarrassed when he returned to the table, and for the rest of dinner that night, it was awkward.

Gossip and backbiting come from the well of pride and ego that hides in our hearts. Jesus said in Mark 7:20–23 what comes out of a man (or woman), that is the thing that defiles us. He says that from within, or out of the heart of men, proceed evil thoughts, including pride and foolishness.

That night at the dinner table, we were not the only ones to hear her speak ill of her betrothed, but the enemy was listening also. In the fallout of their damaged relationship, every time she spoke harshly against him like that, she gave the enemy fuel to keep the marriage in disorder. Proverbs 27:15 puts it this way: "A continual dripping on a very rainy day and a contentious woman are alike." Ouch!

As wives, every time that we speak against our own husbands, we are speaking against our own marriage and ultimately against ourselves. Even in a dating relationship, if you are not matched correctly, you are wiser to break the relationship than stay in one that you continually complain about.

Imagine building a custom home with your husband. Even if you're not married, you can still build a house! You spec out land and find the perfect spot. You find a blueprint that you love and go to work to make your dream house a reality. You schedule the contractors that you think you need, and they go to work.

First, the front-loaders come and dig out the plot per your specifications, and your cement contractor shows up at his scheduled time and completes the concrete pour, creating the foundation for your house. Next, the carpenters arrive and frame out the house, creating walls, stairways, subfloors, and a roof. Then the electrician and plumbers arrive to lay out the wiring and plumbing lines. Then the exterior walls with insulation, siding, and windows are done. The finished house looks lovely, with tons of curb appeal. You and your husband quickly move in, excited to have a custom home built just for you!

But then a storm comes. Wicked winds bring hail and water against your new house, and at first, you think, *Our house is brand new, strong, and secure. We will be just fine.*

No sooner were those words spoken than a water leak started dripping from the ceiling. As the storm gains strength, the water leak becomes worse, until finally the whole roof caves in, ruining your beautiful furniture, clothes, and dishes. Everything was damaged, causing you both to leave the beautiful house and seek overnight shelter in a nearby hotel.

The next morning, you and your husband return and find that your brand-new house, while the structure still stood, was badly damaged from the storm. The interior of the house still had standing water in it, with extensive damage due to the caved-in roof. You call the roofer to find out what happened. The roofer responds, "I was ready to come install the roof and have all the supplies I needed to complete the job, but you never scheduled me to come."

How many of us women have experienced this level of disappointment, the kind that *we* are personally responsible for? The foundation in the story is God, His Word poured in concrete strong and fast to hold against the storm. The house frame, from the basement walls to the A-frame that creates the structure of the roof... these items represent your husband. Grounded in the foundation that is God, built beautifully with windows and siding that make the house look really special. But the roof was just simple plywood that had been prepared for the roofer to lay tar and shingles; however the wife forgot to schedule the roofer to come. The result was a house that was damaged badly by the storm. The tar and shingles are the wife's covering over the house. The wife had a responsibility to schedule the roofer or to cover her house with prayer and thanksgiving, but her failure to do so allowed the storm to damage the house nearly to obliteration.

How many of us wives do this to our marriages? We are the stewards over our homes; we are the "roof, tar, and shingles," and it is our responsibility to climb up to the roof, check it for damages, repair damaged or missing shingles, and essentially, heal what needs to be healed and strengthen what needs to be strengthened by covering it with prayer, blessings, and God's Word constantly. Our failure as wives to do this, whether by ignorance or rebellion, is to the detriment of our marriages. And if you are single, a single mother, or a widow, don't think for a second that you have no responsibility here; on the contrary, it is even more important to cover your house because you fill all the roles in it! Alone, *you* are the structure, firmly seated in Christ, the foundation. You are also the covering—the roof. Your job is even tougher because both responsibilities fall on your shoulders, making it even more critical that you stay in God's Word and let Him strengthen you.

You and I worked hard for our marriages and our children. If you are a single mother, you've worked even harder! And yes, I can say that from experience. My first marriage lasted one week shy of six years, and I was a single mother for 15 years. My first husband stepped out on our marriage, so while it is easy enough for me to judge him for that, I share in the responsibility of the broken marriage. Even though I was faithful outwardly, I was grumbling against him in my heart daily. I talked badly about him to myself, because of his infidelity. I was hurt because I did not feel woman enough to keep him home, wondering what was wrong with me. While I was not to blame for his unfaithfulness, I was to blame for being contentious, always calling out was wrong, and always being quick to nitpick and nag over every little thing that I felt he did wrong. With each infidelity, I became increasingly angry and critical.

Ultimately, we wronged each other and have since forgiven each other of our sins against one another. The result is that we never say anything bad about each other in the presence of our daughter, and God willing, she will marry God's choice for her and learn from my mistakes, to honor her home by being that roof, covering her marriage in prayer.

Today my ex-husband and I have a mutual respect for each other and refuse to allow hate to have a foothold, but it took years of heartbreak to get there. Proverbs 21:9 says that it is "better to dwell in a corner of a housetop than in a house shared with a contentious woman." I am quite certain that my ex-husband would agree that my contentiousness was at least partially responsible for chasing him away.

How is the roof on your house doing? When was the last time you climbed up the ladder of your marriage or your homestead and checked it for damaged or missing shingles? Turn back to God in prayer, over your marriage, over your marriage bed, over your broken heart, and over his broken heart. Believe me when I say that if your heart is broken, you can rest assured that your husband's heart is broken too.

6

BUT I'M STILL ANGRY

I shall allow no man to belittle my soul by making me hate him.

—Booker T. Washington

AFTER MY FIRST TOUR IN GERMANY, I CAME BACK TO THE US and was stationed in Fort Meade, Maryland. It was a great place, with good people and solid leaders. I was experiencing what we now know as post-traumatic stress disorder (PTSD) from my time in Germany, which manifested as anger and rage. Back then, issues like that were kept hush-hush. I had some severe sleep issues and slept with a knife under my pillow.

When I deployed to the Persian Gulf in October of 1990 and remained there until April of 1991, I was already angry. The deployment to the Middle East presented a lot of new issues, some were that could be expected when troops are sent to war, and some that were not foreseen. I went on the deployment for 187 days, first arriving in Riyadh, Saudi Arabia, and then living in the middle of nowhere in tents and sleeping bags until we reached the border of Iraq. We had only the army and packages from home to depend on for supplies and comforts like batteries for our Walkman or books to read. Living in the middle of the desert in tents, we did not have access to stores to shop in, so I saved up a good amount of money while there.

After the war, we came back to the United States, and I went back to Fort Meade, where I was stationed. I went to retrieve my car, which had been in long-term storage along with everybody's vehicles. The people who oversaw the safekeeping of our vehicles while we were on deployment informed me that there had been multiple attempts from a company to repossess my car. I was astonished because I had been deployed to a place where there were no phones, the internet did not exist yet, and we had no contact with the real world. This was the first I'd learned of anything wrong with my car or my car payment. I contacted my lender and learned that they had not received any car payments since October 1990, which is when we left for Saudi Arabia. Prior to the deployment, I had granted my mother power of attorney over my financial affairs so that in my absence, she would be able to make my car payments and meet my other financial obligations.

I placed a long-distance call to my mother to find out why a company had come to repossess my vehicle while I was on deployment. My mother told me that she had used my money to live on while I was gone. To my disappointment, my mother and stepdad had taken every penny. They completely cleaned me out, savings and all. Was I angry? You bet I was. But strange as it may sound, I lacked the courage to confront her about it, so I said nothing. It was weird because here I am back from the war and still afraid of my mom. Still unable to find my voice whenever she was concerned. Still a doormat.

I don't know that there are words in the English dictionary that could quite capture an accurate description of how I felt at that time. Betrayed, lied to, used, angry—the list goes on. I had trusted her with what I thought was a very simple task when, in the end, I was just a source of income for them. I never did ask for the money back, and it took me over two decades to forgive them for siphoning, no stealing, my income. The incident was never to be repeated as I never trusted my mother with my finances again, but that didn't stop them from continuing to ask me for money over the years that followed. I don't know how they managed to stay broke, but they always seemed to run low on money, and eventually, I realized that I was their bankroll.

Fast forward a few years later when I get married, have a child, get divorced, and finally move back to Colorado into a great career in information technology. I had established myself as an expert in my field, made a very good income, and was able to support myself and my daughter as a single mother at the top of her game. I owned my own home and two vehicles and enjoyed having the perks that go with it. All those years that I was doing so well financially, my mother and stepfather continued to ask for money, and I finally became weary of it.

In my mind, there was only one way to make them stop asking, and that was to step away from the resource that allowed me to have such an excess of funds. Why didn't I just tell them no? I couldn't. I can't explain it; I just couldn't say no to them, and I think they took advantage of that.

I ended up quitting my job and lived off my savings account for nearly a year while I went to work for my church. The pay was not nearly as lucrative to what I earned in my prior position, but I loved supporting the IT shop for my church. Unfortunately, quitting my high-paying job was an emotional decision and not at all planned out. I also lost two very close friends of mine, who were killed in a car crash, and with my parents constantly asking for money, it was too much; I cracked. I ended up falling on some bad financial times. I foreclosed on my house, filed for bankruptcy, and lost my car. I even lost some self-respect through the whole process. I was at a very low point because I felt like my only contribution to my family was what I could give in money, and I had no other value than that. While working for my church, I had a low income and no means to supply an unrestricted cash flow. I could finally say no to my parents and mean it. There was no money.

During this time, I dove headfirst into my Bible. In fact, this period of my life is when this book that you are reading right now was first outlined for me by the Holy Spirit. My parents were quite angry with me for leaving my high-paying job and losing my house, financial standings, and good credit. I don't know why they were so angry; it was my life, after all. But with the decreased income and financial loss that I went through, we had a huge falling out. I did finally manage to get a job doing loss prevention for a local retailer, but I had to hitch a ride with my new boss to get back and forth to work; I needed a car desperately.

I asked my parents if I could borrow their vehicle, which was a third vehicle for them and an extra. My mother gave me permission to use the car until I could afford to buy one for myself but then retracted that offer within a couple of hours. She told me that she and my stepdad decided to not let me borrow the car and wanted me to figure it out for myself. I felt a little salty since, for years, I had helped them financially whenever they needed it. But the truth was I got myself into this mess, and it was up to me to get myself out of it, so I'm glad for their refusal.

During this time, I was at my lowest point and God was dealing with me on tithing. I shared with you earlier about God's goodness and His answer to my prayer in that he blessed me by providing me with a car free and clear.

My life was starting to make a comeback, and I was working full-time again. I was able to get to the school to pick my daughter up every day, and I was able to buy more than one bagful of groceries at a time because I didn't have to take the bus anymore.

My new job was great, but the hours were kind of late sometimes, and I would occasionally ask my mother to watch my daughter, who was seven years old at the time. One night at work, something came up that was rather important, and I was unable to leave until about 11:00 that night. When I finally did get to my parents' house to pick up my daughter, my mother and my stepdad had it out with me.

My stepdad told me in no uncertain terms that God had left me. He told me that I had everything, and now I had nothing and would never be more than a welfare rat. He and my mother both told me that just because I went to a church and made a few of them men happy and they gave me a car in exchange for that service, I had no business calling that a miracle of God. They had taken my cry to God and God's good blessing and turned it into something so perverted and twisted. I think some of the anger was coming from a place of jealousy of the blessings over me and my daughter. I'll never know fully why he wanted to turn God's provision for me into something so terrible, except that the enemy will use anybody and anything as a tool against you and me.

Can I tell you how damaged and hurt that fight left me? And what's worse is they did this in front of my seven-year-old daughter, and to this day, she still remembers it, and has no desire to meet them, ever.

That was the last time I saw my stepfather, and I've only seen my mother once in the years since that fight. They had both said some very hurtful, wicked, and judgmental things to me that night. I have grappled time and time again with forgiveness because, in so many ways, I'm still angry with them for using me and stealing from me, with my stepfather for sexually molesting me when I was 14, and with my mother for not protecting me, for not being the parents that I needed them to be, for not loving me. All they knew was that the Bank of Anna was permanently closed, and it ticked them off.

Years later, I was finally able to forgive my mother and my stepfather for all of it, but I can tell you it has taken decades of crying out to God. Why so long? I still had that hurt, that rejection, and the memories of being assaulted on the throne of my mind. Eventually, when I finally took those thoughts captive, and brought them to God in prayer, and released my mom and stepdad in the name of Jesus, those events, the loss of all the money and self-worth, those things no longer hurt me. Whenever they are recalled in memory, I choose to give them right back to the enemy. I forgave my mother and stepfather.

When the enemy tries to attack me with those memories, I don't get angry anymore because I forgave them. I don't get heart palpitations, nervousness, or anxiety. I pray about it and then I release it right back to God. I consciously have to choose to keep God on the throne of my mind, and to do that, I have to actively call my thoughts captive. This is not possible without having a relationship with Jesus, and because of Jesus, when thoughts of the hurt and betrayal my parents put me through drift through my mind, I ask God to bless them abundantly. I can also tell you I'm not too keen on jumping back into a full relationship with them. Truth is, I still feel like an outsider in my own family, but I know that God will restore my relationship with them one day.

My mother is Native American, and she had my older brother out of wedlock with my Mexican father. She dropped out of high school at 16 and was forced to get married to my dad. She had me at 19 years old, but their marriage had already fallen apart. She contemplated aborting me but obviously didn't since I'm here now, but she would remind me of it time and time again when I was growing up. She hated my dad, and I think that, in a way, my brother and I were constant reminders of the shame and guilt that resulted from her own poor decisions. Looking at our faces every day and seeing our dad's features in our faces made her aware of the fact that she, too, was a teen pregnancy statistic and high school dropout.

My mother would talk so badly about Mexican people— their culture and language—and forbade my brother and me from speaking Spanish in our home. Whenever my race was required on documents, like when I began working or when I enlisted in the army, she insisted that I list my race as white, although I clearly was not.

My mother married my stepdad when I was eight or nine years old. My brother and stepdad did not get along at all, and eventually, they had it out. When this happened, my mother sided with my stepdad and my brother ran away from home. Years later, when my stepdad started making sexual advances toward me, I never told my mother because I was afraid, she would have turned on me the way she turned on my brother, so I stayed quiet. In the end, I ended up running away just like my brother did.

The question remains, how do you move forward when you are still angry? For many years, I did what most people do when they do not have an active relationship with God: I buried all those feelings and rarely talked about them. I would vent with my best friend, Elizabeth, thank God for her. She bore witness to it all and never judged me, and has remained my closest friend to this day. On the inside, I had deep emotional wounds. Externally, I had a huge chip on my shoulder. When I went into the military, that was finally my chance to be autonomous over my life, to be free to make my own decisions. Little did I know what was in store for me.

I shared with you earlier some of the things that happened at Kriegsfeld. The warrior, the fighter in me, was born there. In basic training, I was still very much a doormat. I remember my first time firing an M16 machine gun, I was so scared of the gun that I cried while I was shooting it. I cried through the fear because failing meant going home to my mother's house, and there was no way I was going to let that happen. By the time I got to my first duty station in Germany, I had been broken and rebuilt, shaped and molded into a bad ass, like most soldiers when they first come out of training. Unfortunately, I was quickly smacked right back into reality by the soldiers at Kriegsfeld, and I learned first-hand just how much they hated having women among their ranks.

So again, I ask, how do you move forward when you are still angry? Can I tell you—this is one of the most difficult but critically important things any of us can ever do in our lifetimes. If you or someone you know has ever been through the wringer like I have, then you know how difficult it is to answer this question. How is forgiveness possible when you are still angry?

I will share with you something that I realized was critical if I was ever going to experience life without bitterness. The future version of you will appreciate the present version of you for forgiving whatever thing has happened. Let me explain. Your future, the ability for you to thrive and enjoy your future, is placed in jeopardy every time you attempt to thrive in the present while there is still unforgiveness of any kind in your heart. The longer you allow the unforgiveness to go on, or fester, the deeper the root goes into your soul. Eventually, it will contaminate everything that comes out of you.

I remember watching a movie with my husband a couple of years ago, and the movie had a scene in which a woman would burn herself repeatedly on her arm with cigarettes whenever she thought about something that would cause her pain. I nearly had a nervous breakdown watching that film — more specifically, that scene — because as a baby, I remembered my aunt and my mother getting high and one of them put their cigarette out on my hip. The physical scar is still there, but I had not thought about that memory in at least 40 years.

When I sat down to watch the movie with my husband, I did not expect to have a nervous breakdown, but those images triggered the memory of the fact that this had occurred when I was still an innocent child. Now that I was faced with this memory, I could either forgive them in their ignorance and give it to God, or I could throw on my "victim here" t-shirt, treat my husband badly, and create ways for everyone to feel sorry for me.

My husband knew immediately that something was wrong because of my body language, the tone in my speech, and the fact that I suddenly needed to go clean everything. I shared the memory with him, and he was precious, loving, and willing to listen and hold me.

I'm telling you, if you leave these issues unchecked and un-forgiven, they will come back at some point in your life in a way you do not expect and destroy you if you allow it. When God brings these issues to your mind, it is okay to acknowledge the thought, just don't let it take control of you. Start praying about it and bring it to God immediately. Forgiveness can be a compli-cated process, and memories will come up at the absolute strang-est times, when you least expect it, like they did for me with that cigarette burning. Take steps every day to pray about the issue and ask God to reveal how you should manage it. Do you need to forgive someone, or do you need their forgiveness? Ask God to show you how to move forward. He will answer, so listen for that quiet voice.

This can be a very painful process, but I promise that if you act to make it right, forgive whoever it was that did you wrong, or seek forgiveness from those you've wronged, you will thrive in the next moment, in the next day, in the next week, in the next month, and in the next year.

Holding on to what they did to you will never change the facts of what happened. But it also does not entitle you to mis-treat people because of your pain. Hurting people hurt people. And while I was justified in my anger for what they did to me when I was just a baby, I was not justified in holding it against them and living bitter and in unforgiveness, with my sweet hus-band to carry the brunt of my anger.

All the mean, nasty things that have happened to me in my life are just a drop in the bucket compared to the mean and nasty things I have done to my Creator. When I asked Jesus to forgive me for my trespasses and He forgave me, I then accepted the re-sponsibility of also forgiving those who would trespass against me. So, while you also are justified in your anger and hurt, you are not justified in your unforgiveness. The sooner you do for-give and release those people that have wronged you, the sooner the blessings will start pouring themselves out on your head like a monsoon.

Thoughts to remember:

1. Forgiving one another is as important as God forgiving us of our sins. It is so important that we are commanded to forgive each other's trespasses. Look at Matthew 6:9–13. Jesus said, "In this manner, therefore, pray: Our Father in heaven, hallowed be Your name. Your kingdom come. Your will be done on earth as it is in heaven. Give us this day our daily bread. And forgive us our debts, as we forgive our debtors. And do not lead us into temptation, but deliver us from the evil one. For Yours is the kingdom and the power and the glory forever. Amen."

2. Guard your tongue from complaining, grumbling, and backbiting. If a rumor falls into your lap, let it rest with you and repeat it no more. "Hatred stirs up strife, but love covers all sins" (Prov. 10:12).

3. Some hurts can take years and even decades before we are ready to forgive them. When the thought or memory comes, go to work with prayer. Deep dive with your Bible and allow God to lead the conversation that you have internally.

PART 3

LET'S TALK ABOUT SEX

7

NUTS AND BOLTS

THERE COMES A TIME IN EVERY GIRL'S LIFE WHEN WE start dreaming about growing up and who we are going to marry, what our wedding dress will look like, how many brides-maids we will have, and what kind of flowers will be there—at some point, we eventually get around to the groom. We ladies dream about every detail of what our wedding will be like. We can be so committed to planning our wedding, spending our valuable time looking at magazines and websites, wedding gowns, venues, and on and on. We plan every detail to make it a grand affair worthy of a princess.

My first wedding was like that. My first husband and I were both in the army. We had a formal, full military honors wedding; all the men were in dress blues and carried highly shined sabers. When the ceremony was over, we walked down the aisle to-gether under an arc of sabers. Unfortunately, more planning went into that wedding than ever went into the marriage. My ex-husband and I met at Fort Carson, Colorado. We had a physical attraction to one another, and the sex was quite satisfying. We did not love each other at first; we lusted each other. Unfortu-nately, we fraternized, meaning I was a sergeant at the time, and he was a lieutenant in my chain of command. We were given a choice by the senior leadership at the time: either marry or we both would be out of our careers. We married, lightning fast. At some point in the relationship, love surfaced, and we conceived our daughter, but it quickly disappeared after she was born.

Ultimately, he stepped out on our marriage with other women, and I stepped out on our marriage in my heart. In truth, we married one another because we enjoyed sex together, but we did not *know* each other as people. Sure, we had plenty in common, and we both seemed to be ideal in character, but when it came down to it, our physical compatibility is where our common ground ended. The hardest part about that marriage is that not only did we marry for the wrong reasons, but we lied to each other and to ourselves. He was oil and I was water, two substances that do not mix well, and anytime you try to shake them together in a container, they will always separate. How many marriages do you know are also like oil and water? Were you ever involved in a marriage like that?

God is not stupid nor blind about sex. Although we engage in it freely, with whom we want and when we want, we do not expect any consequences for our actions. Even as Christians, we women are not only duped easily, but we can also manipulate men to do what we want quite easily and with the skill of a surgeon.

1 Corinthians 6:12 tells us that "all things are lawful for me but not all things are not helpful." This means that even though nobody is going to come and arrest you for having a sexual relationship with another consenting adult, it does not necessarily mean that it is a healthy choice for you or me. 1 Corinthians 6:13 further goes on to say that we should avoid "sexual immorality."

But what does it mean to be sexually immoral? I mean, in 2022, women have won the right to vote, have equal wages, and lead countries. Then surely, sexually, we should be able to do whatever we want with whomever we want, without accountability, just like men, right?

Any thesaurus would suggest that to be sexual would mean being sensual, erotic, or carnal. Immoral means depraved, dishonest, iniquitous, or corrupt. Joining these two words together makes it sound like something quite dangerous. But surely God understands the world we live in today and that we are so far advanced from two thousand years ago, right? I mean, does God really expect abstinence? We are grown adults, after all, and the last thing you or I want to hear is someone preaching about not having sex outside of marriage. Would you buy a car without test-driving it? And a car is not nearly as big of an investment as a marriage. Besides, who am I hurting? We are just having fun. The excuses go on and on.

I had made that same argument with God too. Even though you may justify that sexual relationship with very sound reasoning, God is not fooled nor convinced. As women of God, He tells us in Proverbs 2:10–11 that "when wisdom enters your heart and knowledge is pleasant to your soul, discretion will preserve you; understanding will keep you."

This scripture also comes with a stern warning. If we leave the paths of uprightness to walk in the ways of darkness. If we rejoice in doing evil and delight in the perversity of the wicked, if we forget the covenant of God, in Proverbs 2:22, Solomon writes, "the wicked will be cut off from the earth, and the unfaithful will be uprooted from it."

In other words, we choose, willingly, to leave God in exchange for the comfort of a significant other. God cannot bless you and me in this type of relationship, no matter how much you plead with Him. If the relationship was born on immoral ground, and you pursue it until it becomes marriage, you will face opposition. God wants you to have that relationship, but in His timing and with His choice for you. God created you; He knows every single secret you keep. He also knows what you need in a marriage partner.

Today the pornographic industry is worth billions of dollars. Why? What is it that draws people by the thousands if not millions? What about this industry continues to draw us away from God in our hearts? If we think that sexual fulfillment is packaged in a box of condoms, in adult films, or in the backseat

GETTING REAL WITH GOD

of the car, not only is God aware of what you are doing, but your actions grieve His Spirit. What does that mean... to grieve His Spirit?

In Ephesians 4:30–31, we read, "And do not grieve the Holy Spirit of God, by whom you were sealed for the day of redemption; let all bitterness, wrath, anger, clamor, and evil speaking be put away from you, with all malice." We give place to the devil when we keep hold of bitterness, wrath, anger, clamor, and evil speech... all of which are by-products of sexually immoral relationships.

When we meet someone new, regardless of the relationship, we make constant judgments, always trying to find common ground first; we search for a way to help each other. In the case of meeting a potential dating partner, we check for wedding rings and ask probing questions to determine whether they're single, married, engaged to be married, divorced, or even widowed. We look and listen for clues that reveal their character, and within the first few seconds, we have already reached several decisions about them. Whether we are attracted physically or not is the main decision, then we quickly assess whether sexual chemistry is present, and if there is, well then, we go to work to harness it and make it ours. We then look at that person for fulfillment and allow ourselves to go into a sexual relationship that we are not emotionally ready to be in. Superficially, it's on; but when we proceed with only the superficial, you and I are setting ourselves up for disaster, willingly entering a sexual relationship with someone that we don't actually know. What's worse is that we women have a superpower; it's called manipulation. And we are excellent at using it.

After my divorce that first year, I was angry. In fact, most women that I know personally or through friends who have gone through a divorce spent that first year so angry and betrayed, with hurt feelings, a bruised ego, and badly in need of healing.

Unfortunately, newly divorced women can be quite toxic and bitter. If you are in your first year of a divorce, do yourself a favor and stay away from dating completely. Your future self will thank you! At least stay away from dating until you have made it past that initial fall-out with the emotional bruises that come from divorce. In that first year, you are so vulnerable, and Satan is keen on this, watching and waiting for his chance to destroy you.

During the first year that I was divorced, I dated a man whom I like to refer to as Satan's brother. He was a silver-tongued prince, and I was emotionally damaged. I was broken, hurt, let down by the constructs of marriage, and I was trying to figure out a way to pick myself up out of it. Getting involved with anybody at that time was a mistake. But I did not date just anyone. No, I had to go for the bad boy. How many of us beautiful, broken women have a built-in trajectory for the bad boy?

I look back at that situation and my choices and see my folly as plain as the nose on my face. Just because it was lawful for me to have a physical relationship with him did not mean it was good for me. He had charisma and charm, and his pursuit validated me—I felt like an attractive, desirable woman and dressed the part, playing the role. Although he did not follow God, I bought what he was selling anyway, hook, line, and sinker. Looking back, it was the chase—that is what appealed to me. Him chasing me, me chasing him: it felt good, felt alive, but it also put me in situations that now, looking back, I realize were risky and dangerous.

He was an alcoholic, and I enabled him. If he had access to liquor, he was happy. No liquor, no happy. I was willing to put up with it, even to the extent of letting him drive drunk, not realizing the danger it put us both in. I did not know that he had been arrested twice before for drunk driving. Luckily, I was not with him when he was arrested the third time. The breakup was ugly, but it was the wake-up call I needed because I was playing with fire.

Not only was I divorced, angry, and a single parent, but I was also emotionally damaged and vulnerable, and he took advantage of that. I was quite blind to the reality of who he really was in character because I was not interested in who he was as a person so much as I was interested in what he could give me, which was acceptance. My desire for that carnal relationship was stronger than my desire to heal. When we finally went our separate ways, it was a good thing on many levels.

In 2 Corinthians 12:7–10, the apostle Paul talks about a thorn in the flesh that was given to him. He referred to it as a messenger of Satan to buffet him lest he be exalted above measure. Paul said that when he prayed to the Lord three different times that the thorn might be removed from him, God came back and told him, "My grace is sufficient for you, for My strength is made perfect in weakness." It is so easy to think that you and I could just say, "Hey God, take this from me," and poof, God will take it away. But instead, God answers us back the same way He answers Paul: "My grace is sufficient for you."

As women, we are way too stubborn to wait and let God's grace be sufficient. We want to microwave what God puts in the crock pot. We gals tend to jump at a moment's notice when it comes to relationships, especially when sex, or the thorn, is involved. Then after the big breakup, we overthink the issue, examining the thorn thoroughly, turning it backward, sideways, inside out, outside in, upside down, and right side up. We go in so many different directions and choose to turn away from God's guidance, thinking we know better. Eventually, we come back to God with it, usually after our heart has been broken again, seeking His forgiveness for not listening for His answer in the first place. For not being willing to accept that His grace really is sufficient for us. We women fall into sexual relationships just as frequently and as easily as men do, and that's the reality. We purposefully hide what we do and remain in secret so that nobody can see our shame or depreciated heart.

God asks us in Jeremiah 23:23–24, "Am I a God near at hand, says the Lord, and not a God far off? Can anyone hide himself in secret places so I shall not see him? Says the Lord, do I not fill heaven and earth?" God sees everything: at the club, meeting up for the booty call, surfing the porn site in the middle of the night, hanging out on dating sites, and even sexting that bad boy, even though you know he is not good for you, but you can't seem to stop yourself. God is also there when you overspend and max out your credit cards, are not paying your bills or taxes, and when you miss your tithe. He even sees when you tip your server at the restaurant. Even if your activities are in the cover of night, He still sees it. If you are stepping out on your own marriage or maybe fooling around with a guy who is married to somebody else, or you have an addiction to pornography, or maybe you make a living in the adult entertainment industry, or maybe you are involved in things that are too racy for me to list—*God sees everything.*

He knows you are hurting, but do *you* know you're hurting? Are you willing to admit you could use a little bit of help? We all have an emptiness, a strong desire to be loved by that special one person that's our match, and in our search to find the perfect husband, we do some of the dumbest things. Even though all things are lawful for you, it does not necessarily mean that those things are helpful for you.

If you are hurting or struggling, whether you are in a season of singleness or in a lonely marriage, you are not alone. Before you were formed in your mother's womb, He chose you—yes *you.* Have you thought about choosing Him instead of giving way to carnal desires? God knows the things that you really want deep in your heart. He is ready and willing to bring those things into your life, but obedience to Him is so important that the more you put it off, the longer it will take you to break those self-destructive behaviors.

Satan's goal is to keep you small and quiet. He uses your bad decisions to taunt you, convincing you that you are not worth God's time or attention and that you are too foregone for help.

> **The reality is that you are the only one who is getting hurt by seeking healing for your soul from men.**

You may not think that you are worth being redeemed, but I can assure you that you are worth so much to God that He calls you His "jewel" in Malachi 3:16–17. You really are that important to God. You are worth dying for, and He proved that to you when Jesus was on the cross *for you*.

8

PURITY VS. SENSUALITY

*Your ordinary acts of love and hope point to the extraor-
dinary promise that every human life is of inestimable
value.*

—Desmond Tutu

ARE YOU AWARE THAT THERE ARE THINGS THAT GOD
hates? We frequently hear about how God loves us in John 3:16:
"For God so loved the world that He gave His only begotten Son,
that whoever believes in Him should not perish but have everlasting life." After reading that scripture, it is difficult to think
that you or I could do something that God hates. After all, it's
such a strong word to use, hate. But if you have children, relatives, parents, siblings, etc., I am sure if you really think about it,
you will find something that they do that drives you nuts, something you hate. It does not mean you love them less, but that
thing you hate builds a gap between you and that person.

Nevertheless, God loves you, but there are also things that
you and I do that God does hate, and just like our families and
their individual issues, these things that we do also build a gap
between God and us. It is unfortunate that we do this because so

many of us are not even aware that what we are doing is offending God! Let your imagination go wild for a minute. Can you think of what those things could be? Sure, the devil, death, sin… okay, we already know from church and Sunday school that God hates those things.

Solomon wrote about this in Proverbs 6:12–15, about a man that is "a worthless person, a wicked man, walks with a perverse mouth; he winks with his eyes, he shuffles his feet, he points with his fingers; perversity is in his heart, he devises evil continually, he sows discord. Therefore his calamity shall come suddenly; suddenly he shall be broken without remedy."

But wait, there's more. Solomon went on to write specifically about seven things that God considers an abomination in Proverbs 6:16–19. They are:

1. a proud look, namely haughty eyes
2. a lying tongue
3. hands that shed innocent blood
4. a heart that devises wicked plans
5. feet that are swift in running to evil
6. a false witness who speaks lies
7. one who sows discord among brethren

While it can be hard to think that God could hate something, the fact that He does hate these things should be a clue to us to avoid them. If we choose sensuality over purity, we open the door to these seven things, and eventually we become desensitized to them; they become an accepted part of our behavior.

It can be hard to stay away from these things because we women are socialized in a society in which outward appearance is valued above everything else and a moral barometer is a thing of the past. We are groomed to "follow our hearts" and cast-off caution. We are taught all around us, from magazines to movies, what is appealing and attractive in today's world, and then we do our best to mimic those standards, even if it means abandoning our relationship with Christ. We live for likes and hearts on social media, even if it means physically changing our appearance or degrading ourselves and our standards.

The idea of purity goes to the wayside as we transform our natural beauty into the sensual, self-serving goddess surrounded by the endless supply of slinky dresses, extravagant jewelry, strappy high heel shoes, heavy make-up, and fragrant perfumes, all in hopes of meeting the hot guy or the bad boy. Have we turned a blind eye to what God's desire is for us? Have we, instead of serving our God in spirit and truth, become the harlot that Solomon wrote about in Proverbs 7?

Proverbs 7:6–23 reads:

> For at the window of my house
> I looked through my lattice,
> and saw among the simple,
> I perceived among the youths,
> a young man devoid of understanding,
> passing along the street near her corner;
> and he took the path to her house
> in the twilight, in the evening,
> in the black and dark night.
> And there a woman met him,
> with the attire of a harlot, and a crafty heart.
> She was loud and rebellious;
> her feet would not stay at home.
> At times she was outside, at times in the open square,
> lurking at every corner.
> So she caught him and kissed him;
> with an impudent face she said to him:
> "I have peace offerings with me;
> today I have paid my vows.
> So I came out to meet you,
> diligently to seek your face,
> and I have found you.

I have spread my bed with tapestry,
colored coverings of Egyptian linen.
I have perfumed my bed
with myrrh, aloes, and cinnamon.
Come let us take our fill of love until morning;
let us delight ourselves with love.
For my husband is not at home;
he has gone on a long journey;
he has taken a bag of money with him,
and will come home on the appointed day."
With her enticing speech she caused him to yield,
with her flattering lips she seduced him.
Immediately he went after her, as an ox goes to the
    slaughter,
or as a fool to the correction of the stocks,
till an arrow struck his liver.
As a bird hastens to the snare,
he did not know it would cost his life.

You see, as women, you and I have a lot of power when it comes to sex, sensuality, and seduction. We say we were seduced by that guy, but it really is the other way around, if we're honest. We are the one who makes the preparation to step away from God, first in our heart, then in our outward appearance and actions. We may not charge for services rendered in a sexual relationship, but we indeed receive compensation in the form of attention and gifts from men and women alike, swelling up our hearts with pride, and before you know it, we are living a lie all over again.

Herein lies the key differences between purity and sensuality. Purity begins with relationship, first with God, in honesty. You and I are His daughters, with an inheritance in the greatest kingdom ever known. When we worship God in spirit and in truth, His peace frees us from the world's standards. When we accept this peace from our Father, we also accept the responsibility to handle our bodies with care and to be honorable stewards of what He has entrusted us with. In practical application, we not only have the responsibility to guard our brothers' eyes, but we are also accountable for it. Just because it might be lawful to be and dress provocatively does not mean it is good for us.

Sensuality, on the other hand, is what we see on television, social media, movies, the mall, the club — literally everywhere we turn. The behavior that goes with it can turn heads, sure. But considering what we read in Proverbs 7:6–23, I think we can agree that it probably falls into the sensuality category. I know it can be fun to play "dress up," and while it is good for us to maintain what we are stewards of, using our sensuality as a weapon is manipulative. Lord knows I have also wielded that same superpower in the past. But knowing now that God has an opinion about it makes me think twice when I get dressed, or put on my make-up, etc. I choose to protect my brothers' eyes because, while it may not be the popular choice by the world's standards, it is the right one for me.

Remember the story about the woman at the well? John 4:5–30 says that Jesus went to a well in Samaria and sat down. Then a woman from Samaria came to the well to draw water. Jesus said to her, "Give Me a drink."

The woman said to Him, "How is it that You, being a Jew, ask a drink from me, a Samaritan woman?"

Jesus responded to her, "If you *knew* the gift of God and who it is who says to you, 'Give Me a drink,' you would have asked Him, and He would have given you living water."

She replied to Him, "Sir, You have nothing to draw with, and the well is deep. Where then do You get that living water? Are You greater than our father Jacob, who gave us the well and drank from it himself, as well as his sons and his livestock?"

Jesus answered her, "Whoever drinks of this water will thirst again, but whoever drinks of the water that I shall give him will never thirst. But the water that I shall give him will become in him a fountain of water springing up into everlasting life."

The woman said to Him, "Sir, give me this water, that I may not thirst, nor come here to draw."

Jesus said to her, "Go, call your husband, and come here."

"I have no husband," she replied.

Jesus said, "You have well said, 'I have not husband,' for you have had five husbands, and the one whom you now have is not your husband; in that you spoke truly."

She replied, "Sir, I perceive that You are a prophet. Our fathers worshiped on this mountain, and you Jews say that in Jerusalem is the place where one ought to worship."

Jesus said to her, "Woman, believe Me, the hour is coming when you will neither on this mountain, nor in Jerusalem, worship the Father. You worship what you do not know; we know what we worship, for salvation is of the Jews. But the hour is coming, and now is when the true worshippers will worship the Father in spirit and truth; for the Father is seeking such to worship Him. God is Spirit, and those who worship Him must worship in spirit and truth."

The woman replied, "I know that Messiah is coming (who is called Christ). When He comes, He will tell us all things."

Jesus said to her, "I who speak to you am He."

The disciples show up, (earlier they had gone to the city to buy food) finding Jesus at the well, marveling that Jesus was talking with this woman. The woman left her waterpot, went her way into the city, and said to the men, "Come, see a Man who told me all things that I ever did. Could this be the Christ?"

This woman was coming to the well to simply draw water, but scripture tells us that Jesus intentionally went to Samaria. John 4:27–30 says that immediately following His conversation with her, she ran into the city declaring to the men there to "come see a man who told her all things that I ever did." Further in John 4:39, we read that "many of the Samaritans of that city believed in Him because of the word of the woman who testified, 'He told me all that I ever did.'" So when the Samaritans had come to Him, they urged Him to stay with them, and He stayed there for two days. And many more believed because of His own word. They said to the woman, "Now we believe, not because of what you said, for we ourselves have heard Him, and we know that this is indeed the Christ, the Savior of the world" (John 4:42).

This story is a wonderful way to eavesdrop on the conversation, and more importantly, it shows you and me that Jesus chose to first reveal who He was not just to a woman, but to a woman *like* her. Today, we would have called her a slut, a whore, or seducer of men, much like that woman in Proverbs 7:6–23.

The key here is that she was not so far gone that Jesus was not willing to save her. He went out of His way to have this conversation with her. He did not have to, but God loved her as much as He loves you and me. No matter how far down we have fallen, Jesus will still meet you there.

You see, in those days, a woman's husband was not just a man she went to the altar with, had a ceremony, and then lived happily ever after. On the contrary, two flesh becoming one is literal in terms of sex. In 1 Corinthians 6:16, Paul says "or do you not know that he who is joined to a harlot is one body with her? For 'the two,' He says, 'shall become one flesh.'" How many of us women have had five "husbands." Or better yet, how many of us have had more than five?

The point here is that Jesus did not judge her or condemn her. Instead, He knew her sins before He even got to the well. He went there with purpose.

You see, as a woman who also has engaged in those sexually active relationships outside of marriage, I can relate to the woman at the well. Thankfully, Jesus does not judge us when we come to Him in honesty and accept Him as our personal Savior. When you and I came to Him, repented, and asked for His forgiveness, He was quick to forgive. But in becoming a believer, we also accepted the responsibility that comes with being a *steward* of our bodies. Before we became born-again believers, it was difficult to understand or connect the dots when it came to purity vs. sensuality. But now that we know that there is a difference, and we know God has an opinion about it, our responsibility is to honor God with our bodies.

The hardship comes when we push God aside anyway, and with each immoral relationship we willingly take part in, we give one more piece of fuel to the enemy. Satan will use that fuel to torment you, guilt you into years of being broken-hearted, lonely and bitter, condemning you into self-loathing and self-hatred. Taking these relationships to the foot of the cross is the only way to take the enemy's ammunition away. Jesus did not judge the woman at the well, even though He knew her sins before He even spoke with her. He also knows yours, and He knows mine.

The minute you confess these things to Him and ask His forgiveness, two things happen. First, Jesus is quick to forgive you because He loves you. Second, Satan loses his power to torment you. The big question here is can you forgive yourself?

9

DEALING WITH EMOTIONS
AND ROMANCE

A flower cannot live without sunshine, and man cannot live without love.

—Max Muller

JAMES 1:13–15 TALKS ABOUT HOW "BLESSED IS THE MAN who endures temptation." God says that "each one is tempted when he is drawn away by his own desires and is enticed. Then, when desire has conceived, it gives birth to sin; and sin, when it is full-grown, brings forth death." God is serious about the consequences of our actions when we go outside of His grace.

I remember a time when my husband and I were at the camper store. We love to camp and really wanted to change some things about our camper. While we were there, we saw the parking lot where the new campers were, and the "spend all your money now" laser beam pulled us both in. Several hours later, we bought a new fifth wheel that was honestly the nicest camper either of us had ever seen. We could barely afford it, and knew that if we bought it, other things we liked to do, like home improvement projects, would be put off for a few years. In stead of being sensible and waiting, we both got in the "I need this now!" mindset and bought the 5th wheel. Unfortunately, it stretched our budget to its limits because we gave in to the temptation to overspend. We were 'romanced' by the salesman, and the finance guy. We ended up regretting the decision to buy it at that time and wished we had waited for at least another year. We still love it, but it is a financial burden that grieves us both. We knew better, but still chose to buy it.

Romance and relationships often mimic this same experience, buying something you know you don't need, it's nice and shiny, a tad out of the budget, and every month would remind you of the burden it presents in your life. Can you think of a time in your past when you were tempted to do something similar that you knew was questionable and acted on it anyway? What was the result? Do you have guilt about the decision?

Every decision we make has a consequence, good or bad. Every activity you choose to be part of has an outcome. I shared with you earlier that I had gotten pregnant as a teenager. I made one bad decision after another, and Satan used my bad decisions to discourage me for years. My already low self-esteem and lack of self-worth kept me believing that there was no way God could ever forgive me. At one point, I felt I had no purpose for my life and was so depressed I even contemplated suicide.

The truth about my mistakes is that I was drawn away by my own desire to be in sexually immoral relationships. I was just 16 years old and had no clue. How many young women at the age of 16, or even younger, are sexually active today? What age were you when you became sexually active? Going back to James 1:14, says, "But each one is tempted when he is drawn away by his own desires and enticed."

When we act on the physical desires born out of our hearts, we willingly place ourselves in relationships that God cannot bless because we are going after something that is our own desire. A sexually immoral relationship is outside the scope of what is pure. Then when we think we are in love, we pray and ask for God to bless the relationship. But if you begin the relationship on tainted ground, God will not magically clean the ground. He is a Holy God, and no sin, not even yours, is permitted to be in His presence. That is the reason for Jesus' ministry, life, death, and resurrection.

I shared with you the consequences of my teenage years spent in promiscuity. In my case, it resulted in abortion not once but twice. Mine is an extreme example, but in all honesty, there are millions of women out there in every range of age who have dealt with that exact same issue and have an abortion hanging over their heads. Women who successfully hide their decision to abort a child may be able to cover it up and lie to the rest of the world, but certainly they cannot lie to God. Until the matter is brought to the Lord, the enemy will continue to use your poor decision against you, and you will never be free of the condemnation. Every new romance and relationship will be tainted, until you deal with the past, and yes, it's going to hurt. Dealing with your own poor decisions takes courage and grace—courage on your part for bringing it to God and grace from the Father who loved you even while you were still sinning.

The enemy will make you think that you are such a bad person that there is no way God could redeem a woman who had an abortion or slept around. People judge in this way; people will condemn and convict you, call you names, and turn their backs on you. The enemy will use anybody to discourage you by reminding you of how awful you are for taking an innocent life; Satan does this to keep you small and quiet. When I finally came clean with God about my bad decisions, I had to fully surrender the issue in its entirety. That meant when I gave it to God, I gave Him every ounce of my shame, my sorrow for the lost innocent lives, and the lust that pulled me into bad relationships again and again.

When you try to move forward in your life, and the discouraging thoughts come at you, how do you cope with them? How often do you find your mind replaying the relationship ups and downs? What about the thoughts that hit you for no reason? The thoughts that tell you how much of a disappointment you are, and how you will never be good enough. Is there a way turn them off? Whatever the relationship, you had a bond, or connection with that person. This is a concept I refer to as a soul tie. Others would call it the knitting of souls. It means that the bond you established with that person was rooted the more you invested your time and heart in that person, taking the friendship beyond the superficial. When the friendship took root and you developed a deeper connection with that other person, the connection became very strong between you.

Whether it's siblings, relatives, friends, a coworker, a supervisor, a client, a contractor, or a dating partner, in general, any relationship can have a bond or a soul tie. If a soul tie binds you to someone who is toxic, has questionable character, is abusive, or whatever the case may be, you must break that bond, that soul tie, to be free of the relationship. Why? Because we become who we hang around with, even in dating. Hitching your soul to those of questionable integrity, low standards, and high compromise will give Satan a foothold to the door of your heart. If Satan is successful, and you are drawn away by your desires, you take God off the throne of your mind and place that other person on the throne instead. This is just one example of how Satan uses your heart against you.

I shared that I had dated the first year after my divorce and jokingly referenced to the man that I dated as Satan's brother. All joking aside, I formed a bond, a soul tie, with that man, which means I gave Satan permission to have another foothold in my life. Even after that breakup, Satan taunted me, not just about that relationship but about all my relationships with men. Satan used it to continue to torment me with loneliness and feelings of never being good enough. Feelings that even my dad didn't want me and that I had no worth. Men that I had dated over the years were long gone, but the bond, the soul ties still existed, and as a result, feelings of guilt, condemnation, and inferiority used those soul ties like a highway connection to remind me that I would never be good enough to be married again, that I was unlovable.

Even after the bad boy leaves for good, that bond is like a wireless connection that keeps him fresh in your mind. He will pop up at the worst times and cause you and me to do stupid things, like trying to revive the relationship at two in the morning after too much wine. Until you break the soul tie, or sever the bond, this will continue repeatedly. If you don't break the soul tie, it will be a thousand times harder to keep from going back to that bad relationship. This is the cycle that keeps you and I in dead relationships. Maybe you don't go back to that loser, but it will only be a matter of time until you initiate a new relationship with another bad boy to replace him.

Breaking a soul tie is simple but can be difficult when you are dealing with abuse, toxic relationships, and a broken heart. Take your time with this and go at your own pace. This is your healing, and God is ready to help you. In Psalms 4:1 David wrote "Hear me when I call, O God of my righteousness! You have relieved me in my distress; Have mercy on me, and hear my prayer." The prayer below is a guide that I use when I need to bring a soul tie to the Lord:

> Father, I bring this soul tie between myself and _____. Please forgive me for following my own desires, and for looking to them to meet my needs instead of You. I repent of the relationship. If I have made any agreements with Satan because of this soul-tie, I break those agreements now in Jesus' name. Please bring this soul tie into Your heavenly court, sever the soul tie and break the bond with the blood of Jesus, and never allow it to return. Bring the soul tie into Your judgment and wash me clean. In Jesus' name, Amen.

You should consider severing any soul tie that Satan uses to torment you, including all areas where you feel small and inferior. The sooner you do this, the sooner you take valuable ammunition away from the enemy. Being diligent in cutting soul ties with every relationship that God brings to you. Eventually, this will deplete the enemy's ammunition stockpile.

In Jeremiah 17:9, we learn that "the heart is deceitful above all things and desperately wicked; who can know it?" How could you or I possibly know that it is our very *heart* that is deceiving us when the world consistently tells us to follow our hearts? I told you earlier about dating right after my divorce. It was my broken heart and subsequent fallout from that relationship that drove me back to church, desperate for answers. I needed to know how people could be so wicked in their hearts. How could someone look so good on the outside and be so decrepit and manipulative once you let them into your heart?

Either you direct your heart, or your heart will direct you.

That first Sunday after the fiery break up with Satan's brother, I started going back to church where the pastor was talking about the heart. Specifically, he taught from Jeremiah 17:9, and it hit the core of my being because I knew that I'd been had by the enemy. I followed my heart, not understanding how deceitful my heart was. I had convinced myself that there was no way that I could make it without a man, that I needed the relationship, needed the validation. I had convinced myself that I needed a sexually active life to get past the divorce. I had convinced myself that even though the last marriage was terrible, the next one was going to be just fine, and I never stopped for one second to examine myself. I never bothered to hold myself accountable for my choices and their results.

That day it all changed when Jesus saved me. I realized that I was perpetuating the cycle that I had been taught by my role models — the same role models we women learn from in the media, movies, TV, school, and in broken homes, like mine. When I finally got real with God about the condition of my heart, He began to change the way I viewed being single and being a single mother. I didn't want this kind of life for my daughter, a revolving door of lovers, so I dove into the Bible and learned how to be an honorable daughter of the God who saved me.

I literally stopped dating, and for the 14 years that followed, I didn't go to bars, I didn't drink, I didn't go hang out with people after work, and I didn't accept invitations to go out to concerts or dance parties because I didn't want to. When I came to the knowledge of who Christ Jesus was, it changed me from the inside out, just like the woman at the well. I realized that I had become just like the other women I hung out with… bitter, cold, unforgiving, and wanting to make their ex-husbands pay for the hurt from the broken marriage. I also realized that I did not hate my ex-husband. I was equally responsible for my marriage failing.

Trying to rebound from a bad marriage with a toxic bachelor was one of the worst decisions I could have made, but God knew how to reach me when I finally opened my heart to Him. I withdrew from friendships that encouraged my sinful lifestyle and *chose* to be involved in church instead. I found toxic people there too, but when I asked Jesus to give me a discerning spirit, He was quick to do so, and I was able to steer clear of them.

When I met Jesus for real, it became so clear to me that when I followed my heart, I set myself up for failure. I was willing to believe anything as long as it "felt right" in my heart and agreed with my ego because I didn't have faith in Him. My unbelief became one of my worst enemies. Coming into a relationship with Jesus cleared the fog around my mind, and I was able to see how Satan used that fog to keep me stumbling in the dark. The heart does not know anything about your future any more than toxic friends who encourage the worldly path. Your heart does not know the intimate things about you that God knows about you. Quite frankly, your heart does not care. Your heart and my heart are deceitful and desperately wicked, but you would never know it.

How many times in movies and television are you and I told to follow our hearts? This is not scriptural! 2 Timothy 3:1–5 says that "in the last days, perilous times are going to come. Men will be lovers of themselves, lovers of money, boasters, proud, blasphemers, disobedient to parents and unthankful, unholy, unloving, unforgiving, slanderers, without self-control, brutal, despisers of good, traitors, headstrong, haughty, lovers of pleasure rather than lovers of God, having a form of godliness but denying its power."

The Bible tells us that we are supposed to turn away from these people, but why is it so difficult to turn away? I believe a lot of us have family members and very close friends who fit the description in the scripture above; I know I do. Sometimes it can be hard to stand by what we know to be true in Christ and stay in a relationship that demands you and I compromise our beliefs. But to keep both relationships healthy, compromise can be our undoing. We become like the people we hang around with, whether we are willing to admit it or not.

2 Timothy 3:6 goes on to talk about "those types of people, who creep into households and make captives of gullible women loaded down with sins, led away by various lusts, always learning and never able to come to the knowledge of the truth." This warning is so important: we must distance ourselves from these people. 2 Timothy 3:8–9 says, "These are men (and women) of corrupt minds, disapproved concerning the faith; but they will progress no further, for their folly will be manifest to all."

What am I saying? When you meet somebody, no matter who they are, ask God for a discerning spirit to keep your heart intact before you jump knee-deep into a new relationship. This will help keep you from repeating the mistakes that Jesus has already freed you from. You have your own mind. You have your own ability to make up your mind. Do not be pressured into something you're not ready for. Remember, God told us that we are not tempted by God.

In fact, James 4:6–10 says that "God resists the proud, and He gives grace to the humble. Therefore, submit to God. Resist the devil and he will flee from you. Draw near to God, and He will draw near to you." The devil will appeal to your loneliness—married or not—your singleness, your attractiveness, your career, and your success or the lack thereof. The devil will tempt you with anything that keeps his foot in the door of your heart. Run. Our good Father would never tempt you.

THE THREE POINTS TO REMEMBER FROM PART III:

1. God knows you have desires to be in a healthy marriage relationship, whether you are married, divorced, a single mom, a widow, or never married. He made you, and He knows exactly what you need to thrive. He knew you before you were formed in your mother's womb. When you and I yield to our own resources to find a marriage partner, we miss some of the key elements that God knows we will need. I know how difficult it is to be patient and wait; I waited for 15 years as a single mom before I married again. I learned that yielding to God and allowing Him to direct your path is not easy, but it is very rewarding.

   If you are married right now but lonely, or single, divorced, or widowed, desiring that marriage relationship, yielding to God does not mean you stop and wait for the solution to drop into your lap. It means staying in prayer about the matter and thanking Him for your husband. Start covering your house, speaking blessings over your husband... even if you are not married yet. If you are married or going through a separation or divorce, God is still in control. You still have a responsibility to pray over your house, especially if you have children. Bring your petition to God. He is waiting for you to come clean with Him. Preparing your life in this way is called faith with works. Do what you can right now and leave the rest up to God.

What do I mean? You can choose to yield control to God and pray over your marriage, over your husband and children, and over your home. Honoring your husband in this way takes work because we ladies always want to take control. The greatest difficulty lies in the control or the lack thereof because it is not just your husband you are fighting. If you are married, you are also fighting against the One who says no man shall separate you two. As a woman who has been through a divorce, 15 years as a single mom, and then remarried, I can speak from experience that control is at the heart of the issue.

Lift your relationship with your husband to God. Honor your husband by putting him first in your prayer life. If certain issues drive a wedge between you and him, pray about those issues *specifically*. James 4:2 says, "You do not have because you do not ask." So, ask! Ask God for insight, for healing, for a quiet tongue, for a desire to keep the peace. When God speaks to you, listen, pray about it, and be diligent to obey the voice of the Lord. You have authority as a wife. This does not make you look weak; on the contrary, it is one of the most loving things you can ever do for your husband and for yourself.

2. We identified what a real bond is, a soul tie, and how the enemy uses them like a highway to your mind. Severing the soul tie shuts that highway down and revokes the all-access pass the enemy has been using to torment you. If this is the first time you are learning about soul ties and why it is important to break them, you didn't know what you didn't know. Now you have a new tool to lock down the hedge of protection around your heart. Use it well, and the enemy will lose his foothold in your heart.

Ask God for a discerning spirit to help you determine if a friendship or dating relationship is going to help you in your walk with God or draw you away from God. If the Holy Spirit lays something on your heart, be quick to obey and follow what the Lord says, especially if you need cut a soul tie.

If you are in a season of singleness, it will all work out just fine. Do the work necessary to prepare for the marriage that will come. If you are married and in a turbulent storm, give the relationship to God and work on your soul ties. Stay in prayer and stay away from toxic people that will steer you away from God.

I remember when my husband and I were bickering a lot, and I had shared my frustrations with a girlfriend, who then told me to leave him. She was also having issues with her husband. Her advice was not only unscriptural, but I could clearly see how the enemy was using her to steer me in my frustrations. I share this with you as an example of who you and I should stay away from. Angry women/girlfriends can be just as toxic to your soul as any misogynist, and sometimes, they can be even worse.

3. We become like the people we hang out with, so if any of your current relationships are keeping you away from God, it might be time to examine the relationship by praying about it and laying it down at the foot of the cross. If you are already in a marriage relationship and in this situation, pray and don't give up. God is in control, He hears you, He loves you, and He needs you to trust Him.

Take an inventory of your circle of friends that you hang out with on a regular basis. If you are the smartest one in the group, finding a new group where you can be challenged to grow and be mentored to the next level will help you in nearly every facet of your life. Trying to level-up any friends, essentially trying to *pull* them up to where you are, will almost always work against you. People, specifically dating partners that are toxic, will just waste your precious time. It is important to surround yourself with men and women alike that will help lift you to the next level in a way that honors God and you. You have already tried sticking it out by staying in the toxic environment that you are in now. You have sat down with your girlfriends and maybe even with your family and complained about how bad everything is.

I am here to tell you, girlfriend, that you have worn the "victim here" t-shirt long enough. God did not choose you to walk through this life to be a perpetual victim, wearing your emotional scars like accessories for your outfit. He chose you, His daughter, to live free from condemnation and guilt. Free from toxic people, free from carnal relationships that profit you nothing. Condemnation and guilt are the ripple effect of our poor decisions.

Why not test God by finding some new friends that help nurture your relationship with the Father? Friends that pour the Word of God into you, like in Proverbs 27:17, where it says, "As iron sharpens iron, so a man sharpens the countenance of his friend."

A word of warning: if you are the toxic friend or the toxic dating partner, like I was, the time has come to change that. How do you know if you're the toxic person? Ask yourself this question: are people happier to see you come into a room or leave the room? Do you have the habit of steering the conversation back to you, or do you listen to others just to listen and be there for them? Do you constantly complain about your hurts, your disappointments, and your battles?

Discarding the perpetual victim mentality takes hard work, but you can do it! Go back to the end of chapter three and work through those exercises as many times as it takes to get free. When I went through that same process, and I finally got real with God about who I was as a woman, and was ready to get over myself and come clean with God about my broken heart, that is when the healing finally started to come, and it will come for you too.

Today is the day for your healing from your past hurts and pain. This is probably one of the most difficult tasks you will ever do. Put in the work, and the future version of you will love you for it. When you are free from the victim mentality, when you get real with God, He will bless you in ways you never expected.

PART 4

SPIRITUAL ROULETTE

10

MAINSTREAM ENTERTAINMENT

...the world is passing away, and the lust of it; but he who does the will of God abides forever.

— 1 John 2:15

IN GENESIS 16:1-6, WE READ ABOUT TWO WOMEN WHO, at the beginning of their relationship, were servant and master but later became equals and then developed into enemies. Do you have any girlfriends like that? Where you started out with the best of intentions for the friendship, but as time went on, you stopped getting along and eventually stopped hanging out with them? What if they are a family member?

The story in Genesis reads,

> Now Sarai, Abram's wife, had borne him no children. And she had an Egyptian maidservant whose name was Hagar. So Sarai said to Abram, "See now, the Lord has restrained me from bearing children. Please, go in to my maid; perhaps I shall obtain

children by her." And Abram heeded the voice of Sarai. Then Sarai, Abram's wife, took Hagar her maid, the Egyptian, and gave her to her husband Abram to be his wife, after Abram had dwelt ten years in the land of Canaan. So he went in to Hagar, and she conceived. And when she saw that she had conceived, her mistress became despised in her eyes.

Then Sarai said to Abram, "My wrong be upon you! I gave my maid into your embrace; and when she saw that she had conceived, I became despised in her eyes. The Lord judge between you and me."

So Abram said to Sarai, "Indeed your maid is in your hand; do to her as you please." And when Sarai dealt harshly with [Hagar], she fled from her presence. (Gen. 16:1-6)

Sarai didn't understand that when God made the promise to Abram years before that he would be the father of many nations, *God didn't need her to accomplish this in her strength*. She was barren at that time, well advanced in age, and decided that she would see God's promise through her thinking, her knowledge, and her skillset. She looked at the physical setbacks of having a child, came up with her solution to God's promise, and brought in another woman to have the child instead of waiting on God to bring it to pass.

Sarai didn't even stop to pray, or think about the consequences, only seeing what she wanted to see and not believing in God's ability to give Abram a child through *her*. She saw herself as too old, not good enough and thought that Hagar, in her youth, was, in essence, a better candidate than she was. She put herself down and gave her handmaiden as a substitute for her husband in order to carry out God's promise.

What Sarai really created was the very first soap opera, full of scandal, bickering, ungratefulness, unfaithfulness, bitterness, and unforgiveness—oh girl, the drama! As if her story was the end of the drama, fast forward a few millennia to current times, and ask yourself, "Is what I see in mainstream entertainment today any different or any better than the drama Sarai created? Does what we watch and accept still cultivate messy situations similar to what happened in Sarai's household when Hagar got pregnant?"

Paul wrote in Ephesians 4:17–19, "This I say, therefore, and testify in the Lord, that you should no longer walk as the rest of the Gentiles walk, in the futility of their mind, having their understanding darkened, being alienated from the life of God, because of the ignorance that is in them, because of the blindness of their heart; who, being past feeling, have given themselves over to lewdness, to work all uncleanness with greediness."

You and I, as followers of Christ Jesus, accepted the responsibility to forgive one another for trespasses when we became His children. But our responsibilities didn't end there. We also accepted the responsibility to no longer be futile in our minds and to stop trying to solve problems that only God can solve.

Paul further explains in Ephesians 6:10–12 that you and I should "be strong in the Lord and in the power of *His* might. Put on the whole armor of God, that you may be able to stand against the wiles of the devil. For we do not wrestle against flesh and blood, but against principalities, against powers, against the rulers of the darkness of this age, against spiritual hosts of wickedness in the heavenly places." Paul is saying here that putting on the armor of God every day will help us when we are faced with battles. Sarai may not have had the armor of God at the time, but she certainly could have turned to God instead of trying to solve the problem in her own strength.

How does Sarai's story relate to mainstream entertainment? We could refer to her as the queen of drama since we see situations like hers mimicked again and again as a staple in storytelling in television shows, movies, and even in social media. Other people's relationships are juicy, intriguing, and full of hooks that keep you and me watching. We spend hours of our lives involved in something that will never yield good fruit. The problems truly begin when we start comparing ourselves with what we see on the screen. We start accepting everything we see in its entirety—the provocative clothing, the make-up, the tiny waistlines, the to-die-for strappy shoes, the rebellious behavior—and we try to make it applicable, adopting the behavior to our everyday lives.

Sarai looked at her handmaiden and began comparing herself to Hagar, and when she did that, she let her pride and ego take over and ushered the drama in. Sarai started picking herself apart; after all, she was old and wrinkled, her youth and beauty fading, while Hagar was young, vibrant, beautiful, and still had a tiny waistline and a sexy body. All Sarai saw was a washed-up has-been with a barren womb and no potential to bring about God's promise to her husband, Abram. She allowed this comparison to distract her from the truth: that she was a blessed mother of nations!

She let the enemy distract her from her task of just being Abram's wife. She gave way to her flesh and her pride, placing her husband in an odd predicament when she offered Hagar to him. I can imagine that when the bickering began between the two women, he probably wanted to be as far away as he could, but here he was, stuck in the middle of the drama.

When you and I watch television and movies, how many of us women stop what we're doing just to see what others are wearing and not wearing? What does their makeup look like? How deep is the plunge on their gowns on the red carpet? Does it stir anything inside of you and me? Do you internally compare what you look like to what you see on the screen? How much of your precious time is spent on this distraction?

Mainstream entertainment reaches even further into our lives through communication devices like our cell phones, including apps that allow us to stay connected to the world around us through social media, texting apps, and any kind of gaming, including those fun little apps on our phones. Add to that mix gambling (especially on the internet). Every one of us is subjected to countless ads that are shoved down our throats, with the media constantly telling us what to think, what to wear, how to talk, and how to act, redefining what sexy really means.

When we bring these distractions into our lives, the line between purity and sensuality becomes extremely blurred and compromise becomes super easy to fall into. Without a secure identity in Christ, every hour we spend on TV, binge shows, movies, social media, and games that encourage questionable behavior and pixelated promiscuity draws us further into the world and away from God.

All of this "beauty" we see on our screens appeals to the greedy little girl we all have inside of us. After all, what girl doesn't want to walk around town, every eye watching us, draped in jewels, in a one-of-a-kind designer dress, flashing those high-end labels at all our friends, letting their envy feed our ego? We've all seen some clothing, shoes, cars, jewels, or make-up and said, "I want to look like that too!"

If it's true that we become what we think about, and what we think about is centered on the superficiality of modern-day media, what then do you and I become? It's one thing to watch TV, movies, and social media content, but a whole other level when it becomes our focal point.

You see, anything that is seated firmly in the world is at odds with Jesus, and if we are not quick to stay grounded in Him, we will let that seed into our minds. It's the seed that says women need to weigh a certain amount to be desirable, have a certain hairstyle to be cool, wear certain jewelry to look hip, and wear their makeup a certain way, by the world's standards, to fit in and be beautiful. Accentuating the beauty that God gave you is part of life, but it becomes an idol in your heart when you focus on your imperfections in yourself instead of focusing on God.

It's so tempting to change who we are to fit into the mold that the entertainment industry says is beautiful. We start seeing the woman in the mirror as less than enough, and in place of our identity in Christ, we see imperfection, too short, too tall, too skinny, too fat, too dark, too light... the list goes on. What's worse is that the battle doesn't end with you.

Your children are also taking notes from you and from society, accepting entertainment definitions of pretty. They will also go to work to fit the world's mold as well. You were wonderfully and fearfully made by God. You are already exactly who God intended you to be, and your imperfections are part of the total package. My friend, you can choose to stop striving with God in this. You've done the work to clearly see your identity in Christ, but you keep hearing the world telling you it's not enough. By God's standard, the only standard that counts, you are enough right where you are. God does not ask you to become perfect to be near Him. He asks you to accept yourself as His daughter. Warts, freckles, curly or straight hair, scars, marks, and tattoos — all of you belongs to Him. His opinion ranks higher because He is God. He made you and me, and He does not make mistakes. You are here on purpose, for a purpose.

Allowing the mainstream media to have a say in this matter will always work against you. Each time you and I allow secular entertainment to tell us what is pretty or acceptable, it draws us away from God one small step at a time. Eventually, we give in to the temptation and willingly step away from our relationship with Christ, becoming indifferent toward Him.

In Proverbs 7:10–11, Solomon talks about a woman, a harlot, and in many ways, I believe mainstream entertainment is just like her. Solomon says, "And there a woman met him, with the attire of a harlot, and a crafty heart. She was loud and rebellious; her feet would not stay at home."

What we see today in mainstream entertainment strives for the shock factor, something that will hook you and keep you watching. Solomon goes on to say in Proverbs 7:21 that "with her enticing speech she caused him to yield, with her flattering lips she seduced him. Immediately he went after her, as an ox goes to the slaughter...." What you and I watch on television and in the movies is enticing and very seductive.

When you and I follow this loud, rebellious woman or look to mainstream media to tell us who we are and where we fit; instead of looking to God, we build a relationship with *her, the harlot,* instead of God. We essentially build an emotional connection to that show, movie, or even a game. When we look to entertainment as our companion, we give it permission to influence our behavior in a manner that does not honor God.

On TV or in movies, we frequently see men and women become involved in situations that cause them to be unfaithful to their spouse, and eventually, we accept it as a social norm: everybody is doing it, so it must be okay. We become indifferent to the behavior and see nothing wrong with it. What entertainment does not show you is that there is a very real consequence of that behavior. What's worse is that our relationship with the loud, rebellious woman will rub off on our children, and you and I are accountable to God for what we teach and for what we don't teach our kids.

The hidden agenda of mainstream entertainment is to distract you and me from reality, and I think we can all agree that it does a world-class job. Not only do we all have 500 channels of junk food for the mind, but we fill in any extra time with games, internet surfing, and social media on our phones and computers, all cleverly designed to distract us from what really matters.

Any tool that can be used to distract you and me from accountability, the enemy will use against you. Remember, the enemy is here to steal from you—stealing your time from critical relationships, like the teenager spending every night on a gaming system or social media feeds where they are drawn away from you, following their own desires. Or enticing and romancing your spouse away with provocative images in a show. Or the young woman seeing those same provocative images, learning that rebellious, sensual behavior is how she should conduct herself in the world. When we allow the entertainment industry to raise our children and influence our spouses and ourselves, we give Satan the permission he needs to steal our children and our marriages from us.

This is a cycle that we can say no to. We can choose differently. God never promised we would live a carefree life, never having to deal with opposition. On the contrary, God does promise that He will be with us *in* the storm. By putting the loud, rebellious woman on notice and turning off the mainstream media in your home, you and I can take back our children and take back our marriage in the authority that Christ gives us.

A few years back, my adult daughter and I strengthened our relationship by doing a digital fast for a week. Rather than post about something, we brought it to one another to talk about, just her and I. Normally, we would have been posting stuff on social media and wait for comments from our friends and family, but instead, we just talked about it. It was a great bonding time with her, and it made a huge difference in our relationship, renewing our mutual respect as women. We also learned that not everything you see on the internet is gold or needs to be posted for the whole world to see.

What kind of movies or television shows do you enjoy watching? I know with just about any type of streaming or cable service, you can get hundreds of different channels, and today you could probably a la carte whatever you like based on what you enjoy watching. What types of programming do you see out there today besides the news, of course? Lots of comedy and romantic comedy shows too. Of all the programming available to you, what do you think has the highest ratings?

I don't mean the highest ratings outside of your house but the highest ratings *inside* your house. What are the shows that you record to your DVR, the shows you absolutely cannot miss? What types of shows do your kids watch? When it's family night, when you sit down together with a big bowl of popcorn, what do you sit down to watch together? What type of content are you watching, and how is it provoking your thought life? What kind of emotional response does the program elicit from your family?

Personally, I like a good romance. *Pride and Prejudice* has always been and will always be my favorite movie, and yes, I'm a romantic. Seeing the underdog finally find love has always struck a chord with me because I guess, in some ways, I saw myself as an underdog who would eventually find her true love and live happily ever after, and for the most part, that's true. I'm still waiting for the happily ever after, for as you well know, if you are married, or ever have been, marriage is a work in its own class!

The big question here is how does the enemy use modern media against you? We know the enemy has come to steal, kill, and destroy, right? So it's a fair question to ask: if the enemy attacks you in your identity and in your relationships, why would he leave you alone when you are relaxing, watching a movie, or playing a game when you're not necessarily on your guard?

In some cases, the enemy is extremely subtle, and in other cases, he's extremely obvious. There are plenty of shows and movies out there with zombies, vampires, the apocalypse, death, and mayhem. But there are also plenty of shows that demonstrate worldly standards for relationship choices, clothing, inappropriate behavior, and attitudes displayed in these shows that are in-your-face rebellious.

If the life rule of "birds of a feather flock together" is true, then what does that say about the shows we choose to watch? How many reality shows out there show the real consequences of people's choices, giving us the benefit of the big picture?

Back in the 80s, we argued about how supermodels on magazine covers were airbrushed to perfection and that real women looked nothing like what we saw in edited magazines. In today's media, the ability to manipulate a picture, no matter where it is viewed, is as easy as downloading an app to your phone and editing the image. What's worse is that our children are sponges, and they're learning everything about the world they live in *through* the world they live in instead of learning from their parents. What you have on the television screen goes straight into their developing memory banks.

Adolescence is tough enough with the hormones, pimples, and oily skin. Being Gen Xers, we did not have to live in front of a world stage. We did not have social media to document our lives, but unfortunately, our children do, and their pictures are out there to be ridiculed by the world's bullies. It's not just us as mothers, sisters, aunts, and grandmothers that the enemy is after. He is after your kids, and the social media platforms that are available today present a whole new level of tools that the enemy will use against you and your family.

Everything your children see that surrounds them, including what is on that television screen, pours into your kids and teaches them life lessons with your consent. If you are not molding them, then the enemy will. Remember that the enemy is not here just to steal, kill, and destroy you, your job, your career, and your marriage, but he's also here to steal, kill, and destroy your children, the next generation of believers, before they can start making a difference for God in the world.

If you are a follower of Christ, then you are on Satan's top ten most-wanted posters, and anybody in your home will be targeted. And if his way to get to you is through your children, well, guess what? That is exactly where he is going to attack you. Solomon told us in Proverbs 22:6, "Train up a child in the way he should go, and when he is old, he will not depart from it." You and I will be held accountable for raising our children; we are responsible for teaching our kids and instilling in them the moral barometer that is fast disappearing in the world.

But what if you don't have any kids? Wherever and whenever there are children around you, just know that they notice everything. The restaurant, the mall, the movie theater, the park, when you are walking your dog, and when you are in a rush in your car and driving like a maniac. You pour into kids because they are everywhere, and if you use vulgar language or display vulgarity around them, believe it or not, you are influencing them to act the same way. And yes, you will be held accountable for your actions.

What you are watching and listening to, you are also taking into your spirit, your inner woman. Do you think these things might have an impact on your outward attitude? Absolutely.

Remember, the enemy likes to use something called distraction. In fact, it is one of his go-to greatest tools of all time. And though we may not always go to our Bible as our first pick for entertainment, anytime we let something into our spirit that isn't good for our spiritual life, we're allowing the enemy to use that distraction to pull us away from God. Essentially, we are giving the enemy our permission to hang out with us for a while. But it is only a matter of time before we find ourselves in another trap. It's like trying to get healthy and eating only junk food.

If we let it go long enough, inevitably, we will go after the desires of our hearts because that's how you and I operate, in the flesh. We know that the heart is deceitful and desperately wicked. Tolerating mainstream media will not help us nurture our relationship with God; on the contrary, it could very well make you indifferent to Him instead.

What am I saying? I believe that indifference comes about when you and I reach a tipping point, question the integrity of someone, and no longer care about their opinion or their influence. We ultimately lose respect for that person.

A husband or wife can become indifferent to their spouse when their heart is lured away by any number of deceptions. A teenager becomes indifferent to a parent that repeatedly makes promises and then breaks them. At some point, the teen will see the repeated let down, the bad habit, and eventually lose respect for that parent, turning to entertainment and their friends instead.

Could it be that when you or I give our attention to spiritual junk food (mainstream entertainment), we give our consent to that thing to lure our hearts away from what really matters, our families? From developing a habit of overspending to watching a show that repeatedly plants seeds of infidelity or materialism, when we yield to what we see in movies and television, we essentially become what we see. We allow entertainment to influence how we conduct ourselves. When we choose to stay in God's Word instead, we become what we take into our spirit and develop the necessary spiritual "muscle" to stay strong.

When we follow the desires of our own hearts, we consume spiritual junk food instead of staying in His Word. This is how we develop an indifference to God. We know He's there in heaven, but when the "honeymoon" phase of the relationship diminishes, the power and freedom we have in Christ become distant and complacent; it becomes more and more difficult to hear His voice. Mainstream media is a tool that the enemy uses to draw us away, romance us away from our Creator. If we take Him off the throne of our minds, it is because we have inevitably replaced Him with something else.

Proverbs 24:1–2 says, "Do not be envious of evil men, nor desire to be with them; for their heart devises violence, and their lips talk of trouble making." If only it were that easy, right? If you've ever fallen for the "bad boy," then you know how difficult it is to stay away from evil men. It goes on to say in Proverbs 24:19–20, "Do not fret because of evildoers, nor be envious of the wicked; for there will be no prospect for the evil man; the lamp of the wicked will be put out."

Either God is on the throne of our minds, or He is not. You and I are daughters of God, and we need a spirit of discernment every day to help us keep God on the throne of our minds. If people are known by their fruits, the things that they do, the decisions they make, and the way they live their lives, you and I are included in that. We also are known by our fruits. Do not pretend to be ignorant of the wicked; God is never fooled and will not let us off the hook if you and I play dumb. Honestly look at the reality of their lives, and you will find that those in the limelight are just as broken as everyone else. They, too, must make decisions and adjustments for their own lives.

11

IDOLS

---

*As long as you want anything very much, especially
more than you want God, it is an idol.*

—A.B. Simpson

EVERY DAY, YOU AND I ARE GIVEN EXACTLY 1,440 NON-
refundable minutes. How do you spend yours? How many of
those minutes do we spend on activities that produce no fruit?
We've all seen it: the awkward silence at the dinner table while
everybody has their face buried in their phones and tablets, preferring their tiny screens over conversation with the people
around the table. Or the countless teens (and adults) that spend
hours upon hours gaming with their virtual friends, people they
don't even know. What about the thousands of housewives who
are bored and alone, surfing the stores online, overspending the
budget on clothes, jewelry, and shoes, looking for ways to get
their sexy back. And the millions of men, women, and yes, teens,
surfing the internet for pornography. And let's not forget the millions of people who are hurting, looking for a way to alleviate
the internal pain by self-soothing with drug addiction. What in
the world is going on?

Idols. Now there's a word you don't hear every day. An object of extreme devotion, or an idol, is something that has come between mankind and God since the days of Adam and Eve. Genesis 3:1–6 recounts the event that changed it all.

> Now the serpent was more cunning than any beast of the field which the Lord God had made. And he said to the woman, "Has God indeed said, 'You shall not eat of every tree of the garden'?"
>
> And the woman said to the serpent, "We may eat the fruit of the trees of the garden; but of the fruit of the tree, which is in the midst of the garden, God has said, 'You shall not eat it, nor shall you touch it, lest you die.'"
>
> Then the serpent said to the woman, "You will not surely die. For God knows that in the day you eat of it your eyes will be opened, and you will be like God, knowing good and evil."
>
> So when the woman saw that the tree was good for food, that it was pleasant to the eyes, and a tree desirable to make one wise, she took of its fruit and ate. She also gave to her husband with her, and he ate.

The first idol, the fruit from that tree, drew a wedge so deep between God and mankind that it permanently severed the relationship between Adam and God. The consequences of Eve's choices can still be felt today in every one of us women.

It's easy to picture: Eve going about her day, coming across the Tree of Life and being challenged by the serpent to eat from it, and being duped into temptation, a choice I'm certain she regretted the instant her eyes were opened, and she realized she was naked. I can picture her beautiful, long, flowy hair, all sparkly-eyed, full of joy and content with her life, married to the man of her dreams. The serpent stops her one day and plants a lie, a seed in her mind that says, "You need more because you need more." That seed takes root in her mind, and she engages in the conversation, the serpent goading her into wanting something she doesn't need. The serpent appeals to her ego, telling Eve that she "wouldn't *surely* die" and that if she ate of the fruit, her eyes would be opened and she would be like God.

Eve starts thinking about what the serpent told her, and her inner dialogue kicks in: "Yeah, the fruit does look good enough to eat, and who wouldn't want to be wise? Maybe I *should* try it."

Eve takes the fruit, eats it, and hands it off to her husband to eat.

There is a *huge* key here that you and I should pay close attention to. When the serpent spoke to her, she *stopped and listened*. The serpent appealed to her ego, her pride, and *being drawn away from God by her own desire*, she came into agreement with the serpent and ate the fruit that God specifically said not to.

In today's world, what does an idol even look like? We don't have access to that Tree of Life like Eve did, but are there other idols that stroke our egos in the same way that the serpent did to Eve? Do we still see idols carved from wood or stone, like in the Old Testament? Or if there are idols around today, what are they made of? Are idols something you can consume? Or is it something you can throw out with the garbage? Is it even tangible?

Realistically, an idol is anything that you or I desire more than we desire God. You and I have a "throne room" in our minds. This is a special place in our inner woman where we focus our attention, our love, and direct our hearts toward whatever is on the throne. As a believer, God should be on this throne all the time. If you and I put other things on this throne too, well, God won't share His throne with it.

Whenever we put something else on that throne, we are choosing to turn away from God and choosing to make that other thing our idol. We essentially allow the idol to encroach God's place on the throne, displacing God. This change in position is why you and I have so many inner arguments with ourselves.

Our flesh wants the idol, and our soul wants the pure relationship with God. When the two contend for the same throne, *you decide* which one wins the battle.

On the throne of our minds, idols exist in all shapes and sizes, in the form of everything from television shows and movies, money, jewels, shoes, land, cars, clothing, computer games, music, books, cell phones, power/control, and even people. We women keep idols alive in our hearts by going after the things our hearts desire without realizing the impact that choice has on our lives and families.

For every action and decision, there will be a consequence, both good and bad. Are you willing to pay the price of keeping an idol on the throne of your mind? Most commonly, idols take the shape of vices, or what is better known as addictions. Weird, right? But not weird to God. Is there an idol on the throne of your mind? An addiction that you keep returning to, trying to hide or quit in your own strength?

When I first got saved as a teenager, I didn't understand anything, and I was already knee-deep in rebellion, so although I went through the motions, I turned my back on Jesus. Fast forward 15 years, when I committed my life to Christ, I was still a smoker. I started smoking when I was a 15-year-old rebel without a clue. I would steal a cigarette here and there from my mother's purse and eventually became addicted. My parents would tell me I wasn't allowed to smoke while they were smoking! Unfortunately, I judged them as hypocrites and kept right on smoking.

Of course, only a smoker or someone with an addiction knows how powerful addiction can be, whether the addiction is to alcohol, illicit or pharmaceutical drugs, gambling, pornography—the list goes on. My addiction to cigarettes controlled me, and as a smoker, my smell and taste became filtered, just like the tobacco. The smell never left my hair or clothes, but I enjoyed smoking; I thought it made me look cool, which appealed to my ego. In my mind, there was nothing more satisfying than having that first puff right after you finish eating a meal. For some reason, it was extremely relaxing to me. But it wasn't good for me, my lungs, or my daughter.

Years later, when I became a newly devoted Christian, I was still smoking. As a single mother who talks about how wonderful Jesus was and how lucky I was to know Him, I was going to church every week with my daughter, and I was still smoking two to three packs a day. It wasn't that other people made me feel judged or like I was a hypocrite; I made me feel like I was a hypocrite because while Jesus had healed my heart, I was still yielding to an idol, my cigarettes. My flesh wanted the addiction, but my spirit wanted Jesus. I knew that every time I lit up a cigarette, I was yielding to the addiction and not yielding to the healing. I started praying in earnest about it, but I did not *accept* the healing from the moment I prayed; I accepted the healing the moment I *yielded in obedience to God.*

God is not a wizard, and He does not come along with a magic wand, wave it over the situation, and bam, suddenly every problem is fixed and we emerge perfect. No, God doesn't work that way. How God does work is that He heals the behavior by *first addressing the rebellious spirit* in us.

Looking back, I can see where my addiction to cigarettes, my idol, controlled me. That's the tricky thing with idols and addiction. It controls the person, but we think we can quit any time because we are in control, which is a lie; the idol is the one who really has control.

I kept God off the throne of my mind and kept nicotine there, but it went deeper than that. I had to acknowledge my agreement with the spirit of rebellion and break that bond, that agreement, in prayer and in Jesus' name. I pursued cigarettes and nicotine because my desire to stay in rebellion and addiction was stronger than my desire to put God on the throne of my mind. I was drawn away from God by my own desires to be socially accepted (ego/pride) and to be disobedient to my parents (rebellion and harboring bitterness). I had willingly aligned myself with sin, and I endorsed my sin every single time I lit up another cigarette.

I was steeped in addiction, meaning I was saturated with the pervading influence of nicotine, by my choice. As a woman in addiction, I was afraid of what life would look like without it. Smoking became a shield in a weird way; I hid behind it, and I wasn't willing to let it go. But more importantly, what I didn't realize, or maybe I realized it and didn't want to come to terms with the truth, was that I didn't smoke necessarily because I enjoyed it, and I didn't smoke because it was something that gave me relaxation. After all, I knew it was gross, was smelly, gave me bad breath, and set a bad example for my daughter. No, I smoked because it was a way for me to keep the rebellious spirit in me satisfied; I yielded to what the addiction in me wanted, even though I knew the source of my addiction was rebellion. When I prayed for healing to overcome my smoking addiction, God had to first address my idol, my rebellious spirit, because it occupied the throne that God rightfully deserved. Once God was back on that throne, the healing, the deliverance from the spirit of nicotine, came, and I never had so much as a jitter, craving, weight gain—nothing. Not a single relapse or side effect that people often get when they try to break that addiction.

When I was delivered from smoking—and yes, I was *delivered* from smoking—I did not just wake up one day and decide to quit. I had to take it up in prayer, earnest prayer for months, and I had to accept responsibility for my actions. I had to confess to God that I was more interested in pleasing myself rather than pleasing God and that I, for years, yielded to my idol, my rebellious spirit, against Him.

I do hope that you grasp this important life-changing key. Anything, whether it's smoking, drugs, alcohol, pornography, sex, anger, gaming, gambling, food, sugar, power and control, family, friends, or even your church, can become an idol if you put it on the throne of your mind. Addictions and the behavior that results from yielding to them all have a root in rebellion against God. Things you would never suspect of becoming an idol can slip in without your consent and take root if you are willing to compromise. When we allow those addictive behaviors to control us, we are nurturing a spirit of rebellion.

When God delivered me from smoking, I did not think I was ready at that moment to be healed. It was in the evening when I was home, my daughter was in bed upstairs, and I had walked out on my back patio to have a cigarette. I sat down, lit up, and took a nice long pull, and that is when I heard God speak so quietly into me. He said, "Put your cigarette out."

"What?" I replied.

God answered me, "It's time for you to put your cigarette out."

I immediately did what we all do when we are held accountable: I started arguing with God. How many of us do that when we hear His voice giving us direction to do something? How many of us argue with God when He speaks, and we don't even realize we are arguing?

Even in the simplest direction from God, like tithing (which I was not doing), my first knee-jerk reaction was, "I have to give up this money? Are You nuts?" Or when you hear God's voice telling you not to make that purchase, that thing you don't need… and the first thing you do is emotionally appeal to God about how much you need it. I do it too. Those to-die-for shoes, that sweet ride, a new camper, that pair of diamond earrings, etc. Things you want but don't necessarily need.

Whatever idols are on the throne of your mind in this moment, and you already know what they are, God will heal you from them, but first He must deal with the rebellion that you yield to every day. For me, it was cigarettes, and when God told me to put out the cigarette that I had just lit, I immediately began to argue with Him. Ask any smoker who just lit a fresh cigarette how difficult it is to put it out. Not just because they are expensive either, but mostly because they want to finish it to the very last bit of tobacco. It's like telling an alcoholic to throw out his beer after one sip. Crazy, right?

The night I was delivered from the spirit of nicotine, God spoke to me quietly, saying, "Put your cigarette out." I still hesitated—I could just kick myself, but I did—I hesitated and started to justify why I couldn't put it out. Then He posed a question to me that was so on point, not just for me but for you too. He asked me, *"Will you obey My voice?"* The conviction that I had at that moment was bigger than anything I had ever felt before. I put my cigarette out and, at His direction, destroyed the entire cigarette by stomping the whole thing into the ground rather than trying to cheat and save it for later.

At His direction, I went back inside to my kitchen. God spoke into my spirit and told me to call my mom and ask her to pray for me right then and there. (This was years before the big fallout with my parents.) I called my mom and asked her to pray for me and with me about the nicotine addiction and the spirit of rebellion. I repented of my rebellion against authority, and I rebuked the spirit of rebellion and nicotine, my idol.

Immediately my mother started praying with me, and the deliverance that followed was amazing. I felt a physical removal from my mouth, like when you remove a plastic wrapper from a package. In Matthew 18:18–20, I'm reminded of Jesus saying, "Again I say to you that if two of you agree on earth concerning anything that they ask, it will be done for them by My Father in heaven. For where two or three are gathered together in My name, I am there in the midst of them."

I know that Jesus healed me from that addiction, and it was because I was (finally) obedient to what the voice of the Lord was telling me to do. It was not how I saw that evening going, but let me tell you that since then, to this very day, I have never craved nor missed a cigarette even once.

God's healing was complete, final, and total. But look at what had to happen before I was healed.

First, I had to take it up in prayer with Him. I had to come clean with Him by acknowledging that, as a smoker, the cigarettes were an emotional crutch to me. I had to repent of the spirit of rebellion and for allowing rebellion to dictate my life. I had been yielding to a spirit that was not from the Father. God wants to heal you this way too, from whatever is your idol. Rebellion was mine. Smoking cigarettes was how my sin, my rebellion, manifested itself in my life, but ultimately it was the spirit of rebellion that had its hold on me.

Second, God's healing was on His timeline, not mine. I wanted God to free me the moment I prayed for help, even though I was not yet ready to accept the healing. Ephesians 6:12 tells us that "we do not wrestle against flesh and blood, but against principalities, against powers, against the rulers of the darkness of this age, against spiritual hosts of wickedness in the heavenly places."

I wanted the healing, but I was not willing to give up the cigarettes themselves because they nurtured my rebellious spirit. I *wanted* to be free of smoking without actually giving it up. How many of us do that doublemindedness thing? My cigarettes, that is, my *addiction* to cigarettes, controlled me. Rebellion was my idol, the thing I kept on the throne of my mind.

The third thing that had to happen before my healing occurred was that I had to pray continually and thank God for the healing, calling out by faith that I was healed already. It was not one of those "one-and-done" things. I had to be in prayer *when* I would smoke a cigarette. I had to claim the healing from the sin *while* I was still in the sin. When God called me that evening to my healing, I had to choose. I could have remained disobedient, but I chose to obey, even though it was on His timeline and not mine. I had to be willing to obey what he was asking me to do in that moment. I could have disobeyed and kept on smoking. There is no law saying I could not, but even though it is not against the law for me to smoke cigarettes, it is not necessarily helpful for me to smoke them either. When I was freed from that addiction, that idol, God sealed the healing, and I have never even had the thought to go back to it.

My question to you is this: is there an idol in your life that lives on the throne of your mind and keeps you in captivity? What does it look like in your day-to-day life? How does the idol contend with God's presence in your life? Can you identify the root of the idol? When God speaks to you about it, do you try to justify it to Him like I did? It could be anything from sex addictions to emotional eating—all of us have sinned and fallen short of the glory of God, and whatever it is that you hide from the world, He already knows about it. You are not alone in this fight. God is present and willing to heal you, but are you willing to let Him?

Here is my go-to prayer when I start seeing another idol try to take over the throne of my mind. Mind you, I am not perfect either, but I can promise that if you bring it to God in spirit and in truth, He will go to work on your healing well before you are ready to receive it.

> *Father God, I recognize You as my Creator, the Lover of my soul. And despite Your love, I've run away from You, drawn away by my own desires. Father, I am sorry for my rebellion and for chasing idols, the things that keep me away from you. Father, please forgive me for my rebellion. If there is an idol still sitting on the throne in my mind, please bring it to the forefront of my mind vividly, so I can address it specifically. Thank you, Father God, for your grace; without You, I am nothing.*
>
> *In Jesus' Name, Amen.*

12

WHEN YOU ARE TEMPTED

Each one is tempted when he is drawn away by his own desires and enticed.

—James 1:14

I BELIEVE THAT GOD IS CALLING ALL HIS DAUGHTERS, IN-cluding you and me, the women at the well. He is asking us to stop walking the way the rest of the world is walking and stop being okay with the compromise and backroom deals with the devil. It's okay to ask questions about what you are taking into your spirit, your inner woman. In fact, I would encourage you to ask questions because you are responsible for being a good steward of what He has given you, including your mind, body, children, husband, and household.

1 Corinthians 10:13 tells us that "no temptation has overtaken you except such as is common to man." Anytime you face a situation that has you yearning for something other than God, remember that He says whatever the temptation, *it is a common problem* to you and me. He is not surprised by it, and you and I shouldn't be surprised either. Verse 13 goes on to say, "But God is faithful, who will not allow you to be tempted beyond what

you are able but, with the temptation, will also make the way of escape, that you may be able to bear it."

There will come a time going forward, perhaps even today, when you're going to come across temptation. It's something that you or I will never escape, but with the right tools and training, you and I can develop the skills we need to successfully honor God. 1 Peter 5:8–9 says that we should "be sober, be vigilant; because your adversary the devil walks about like a roaring lion, seeking whom he may devour. Resist him, steadfast in the faith, knowing that the same sufferings are experienced by your brotherhood in the world."

You are not alone in whatever your vice, temptation, or addiction may be. Be completely honest with yourself and with God, whatever the problem. He will help you more than you know. He already knows the difficulties you've had in this area, and He still loves you despite how imperfect you are.

He took the scales off your eyes and the cotton balls from your ears the day you accepted Jesus as your Lord and Savior. He created a heart of flesh in you and me, and we both are no longer blind in our hearts. Anytime you and I choose to pursue something that we know is not from Him, it is like putting a blindfold over your heart and going after it anyway. No matter where you go, no matter what you do, there is no place that you can hide from the Spirit of the Lord. There is no mountain high enough and there is no ocean deep enough to hide you from God.

If He is speaking to you about something in your life that He wants you to come clean about, talk to Him about it, just like you would talk to me about it. After all, we are sisters in Christ. Shout, scream, cuss, cry—whatever it takes to get your frustrations out of your head and into God's very capable Hands. His desire is that you would come to Him in spirit and in truth, and you can't do that while you are wearing a blindfold over your heart.

I want to encourage you that when you are tempted, you have been supplied with tools to help you overcome it.

Know that God is always near you and that no matter how far you run, He will always find you. He is willing and ready to fight for you. Your ability to let go of your past hurts is within your reach. Here are some of the key areas that were discussed in the earlier chapters of this book.

WORK OUT YOUR IDENTITY IN CHRIST.

God intended for you to be alive at this moment in time, in this life, and He had an intention for you, a purpose, since before you were born. Sometimes you and I can find it difficult to receive our anointing because we do not feel like we are worth it. Maybe we have made too many mistakes and there is no way God can bless us. This is a lie of the enemy.

For those women that are like me, who grew up fatherless and feeling abandoned, the struggle to figure out our identity can take years, even decades. Not knowing who you are can set you up for failure. It is not fair to grow up this way; no child asked to be born. Yet we can be turned out by one parent, sometimes both.

Even for kids who grow up with both parents in their home, figuring out your identity can be one of the most difficult things you'll ever do. I have a friend who grew up with brothers who would bully her constantly. What's worse is her mother and father allowed it, never stepping in to defend her, never instituting correction with her brothers. It was not fair. She did not ask to be born a girl, the weaker sex, but that is how God made her. How many of us have lived through something similar, life with bullies in our own homes?

Maybe you came from a home where you endured years of emotional, mental, and physical abuse like I did. Maybe you have even looked death in the face. Maybe you made bad decisions trying to figure out your own "daddy issues."

Whatever your situation is, if you are a born-again believer and have come into a relationship with Christ Jesus, then your identity is solidly in the Kingdom of God. The moment God forgave you and you accepted that forgiveness and accepted Jesus as your savior, you became His daughter with an inheritance in Him. Your identity is no longer in question, and it is not negotiable.

Accept the fact that not everyone is for you. In fact, there are going to be people who are downright against you from the very beginning of your life. This includes the enemy of your soul, namely Satan. Jesus told us that the enemy is a thief and that he is here to kill, to steal, and to destroy you and me. The only way for the enemy to kill you, steal from you, or destroy you is if you sit idly by and do nothing. God put in you a spirit of a warrior, just like Gideon, who was hiding when God called him to come and fight. Gideon did not see himself as a warrior either, but God knew what He planted in Gideon before Gideon was even born. You can read Gideon's story in Judges 6:11–40. God planted seeds of greatness in you too, and the enemy's goal is to steal, kill, and destroy everything in you, including your greatness.

When those thoughts from the enemy start sailing through your mind that you're not good enough, that you can't do it, that God has left you, you can choose to handle the battle the way Jesus did, with scripture, God's Word. How will you know what scriptures to answer with? Staying in God's Word daily will keep your spirit full of the love of our heavenly Father. Even five minutes make a difference! There are plenty of resources available to you, like my daily Dive Into Proverbs (DIP), which you can sign up to receive via email by going to gettingrealwithgod.com.

When the enemy does send thoughts your way, take that thought captive. Examine it. Measure the thought against God's Word, not the world's standards. Then choose what to do with that thought. And if you choose to give it back, do it as quickly as you can. Do not waste your precious time and energy on something that profits you nothing. The world is not going to cheer you on. But God will.

HE CHOSE YOU; NOW IT IS YOUR TURN TO CHOOSE HIM.

If you step away from the things of the world, the perilous lusts of this age, and instead go after the purpose that God put in you, yes, the enemy is going to try to stop you. And the greater the calling on your life, the more resistance you will face. The enemy is going to try to stop you from becoming everything you were called to be. But you have God in your corner, and you plus God makes the majority.

Stand on that promise, and God will refresh you just like an eagle that rises above the trees, the fog, and the dense foliage where the enemy hides traps from your sight. God will strengthen you and help you see through trees and the fog. Trust that God established your path. Even if the world is against you, you are born of God's spirit, and where He is taking you, the enemy cannot follow.

LEARN TO FORGIVE FREELY AND QUICKLY.

It is easier said than done; however, it is key in receiving all the blessings that God has stored up for you in heaven. If God can't trust you in the small, He is not going to trust you in the great. That means if somebody offends you—say they cut you off in traffic—be quick to forgive them and let it go. But if you fly off the handle and start cussing them out, maybe road rage with them a little bit, don't be quick to just forgive them. Own up to God with your own actions and be quick to ask for His forgiveness.

What God has forgiven you, no one can hold over your head, and that includes you. Stop holding your sins over your head as though you just committed them 10 seconds ago and have never received forgiveness. Your sins are in the past, but now it is time for you to look forward instead of looking back.

Your sins, or skeletons in the closet, cannot hurt you anymore. Come clean with God about your sins and how you have let those memories influence your decisions. When God forgives you of those sins, be quick to forgive yourself too.

GUARD YOUR MOUTH AGAINST HARMFUL SPEECH.

It sounds simple enough, but this is one of the hardest things in life to do. You cannot un-say something. Once words leave your mouth, the damage is done. If gossip is something you fight against, bring it to God. If you go into a bar and truckers come running out because of your foul language, bring it to God.

Jesus said in Mark 7:20–23, "What comes out of a man, that defiles a man. For from within, out of the heart of men, proceed evil thoughts, adulteries, fornications, murders, thefts, covetousness, wickedness, deceit, lewdness, an evil eye, blasphemy, pride, foolishness. All these evil things come from within and defile a man." Proverbs 18:20 says that "a man's stomach shall be satisfied from the fruit of his mouth; from the produce of his lips he shall be filled." Essentially, whatever words we speak demonstrate to everyone around us what is in our hearts. Whatever feelings and emotions you are harboring internally comes out when you speak.

Solomon said it best in Proverbs 15:4 when he said, "A wholesome tongue is a tree of life, but perverseness in it breaks the spirit." You are a daughter of God, and you have an inheritance in heaven and blessings just waiting to be poured out into your life. It is wise to remember that God is not the only one who hears you when you speak, but the enemy also hears you.

While there are times when it may be difficult to use wholesome speech, especially when you're angry, especially when all you want to do is swear at someone, your words are a tree of life to the person who hears it, or your words can break their spirit;

you choose. In Proverbs 15:1, Solomon also said, "A soft answer turns away wrath, but a harsh word stirs up anger." You can choose your words, but if you ever feel like you are going to have word vomit and no control over the things you say, the best thing to do is zip it. Just like that old saying: if you can't say something nice about someone, don't say anything at all. Truly it is better to remain silent and give the appearance of being wise rather than speak and let people around you know otherwise.

EVERYBODY GETS ANGRY, BUT AT WHAT COST?

I have certainly had moments in my life where I handled things poorly and said or did things that I regretted instantly. Has that ever happened to you? There will always be moments when you are disappointed. Maybe somebody let you down, maybe your car broke down, or maybe you heard that somebody was talking about you at work or at school. No matter what the source is, if it makes you angry, believe me, the enemy is going to take that one to the bank. How you choose to react to any given situation shows the character deep inside of you. You are a princess, a daughter of God with a royal inheritance. You may not know this, but you wear a beautiful diamond tiara on top of your head. You may not see it with your eyes, but it is there, rest assured.

There will always come times when somebody is going to make us mad. I have even had days when it started bad, the middle was bad, and the evening was bad, and I simply just needed to redo the entire day. Have you ever had a day like that? Every time you and I fly off the handle and lose composure, our crowns fall right off our heads. The only way to get that tiara back on your head is to go into that prayer locker of yours and give the situation to God. Ask for His forgiveness for any actions that you might have done or things that you might have said that were hurtful to somebody. Then, rather than overthink the scenario 50 million times, just forgive the person who offended you.

Then, forgive yourself and move on. I have had to do this multiple times in a day. As someone who has been diagnosed with PTSD, I found that the trip from calm and peaceful to extreme rage was a very short one. Thankfully, I have learned since then that even though somebody may make me angry, I get to choose if I am going to let their actions or inactions dictate my day. It could be their words, the way they drive, or the way they cut in line at the supermarket. Whatever the offense, I get to choose how I react. I have heard it said this way: a thermometer reacts to the temperature in the room at any given time. But the thermostat is where you set the temperature in the room. Are you a thermostat or are you a thermometer? Thermometers are a dime a dozen; you can have them all over your house. But you only need one thermostat because it sets the temperature for the whole house.

Why is it important to choose to be the thermostat? Because once you have said whatever it is you said, and it hurt or broke the spirit of the person you spoke to, you cannot take those words back. The damage is done, the temperature has been set. The only way to make a comeback from it is to do damage control.

There was a man in the Bible named Jabez; his name literally means "he causes pain." Later in his life, he had the audacity to speak an outrageous prayer to the Lord about causing pain to others. 1 Chronicles 4:9–10 says, "Now Jabez was more honorable than his brothers, and his mother called his name Jabez, saying, 'Because I bore him in pain.' And Jabez called on the God of Israel saying, 'Oh, that You would bless me indeed and enlarge my territory, that Your hand would be with me, and that You would keep me from evil, that I may not cause pain!' So God granted him what he requested."

The last statement in there, *"keep me from evil, that I would not cause pain,"* is a conscious choice that Jabez made when he prayed it. He desired to not hurt others, even though his very name said he would. God had the power to answer Jabez, and He did!

You and I have that same choice right here, right now. We can all benefit from saying this same prayer every day as a constant reminder of how important it is to watch what we say. Your words can either be a tree of life to the hearer, or your words can break their spirit; either way, you and I both will be held accountable for our words. In every instance of your life, you get to choose which one it is.

JUST BECAUSE YOU CAN DOES NOT MEAN THAT YOU SHOULD.

Paul said in 1 Corinthians 6:12 that "all things are lawful for me, but all things are not helpful..." With every decision you make in your life, from clothing to car to dating partner, all decisions have a consequence, good or bad. The consequences that come from being sexually active outside of marriage can sometimes be very defining and life-changing. Consequences come in all shapes and sizes, from unwanted pregnancy to sexually transmitted diseases, divorce, and even heartbreak. It is a huge risk to your future for the sake of being sexually active outside of marriage or with multiple partners.

Whatever your situation, if there are spiritual soul ties that developed from sexual indiscretion, it is very important for you to break the bond, or soul tie that was formed. This is key to your freedom in Christ because if you keep that soul tie open, it is a foothold that Satan will continue to use against you.

When I was a police officer, I did not date. With my work schedule, it was nearly impossible. What I did have was another police officer that worked similar hours, and he and I enjoyed each other's company whenever the opportunity presented itself. Yes, what I am confessing to you is that I had a booty call. We had a secret code word that we would send to each other, and if the timing worked out, we would "hook up." There were

GETTING REAL WITH GOD

no rules against it. He was single, I was single, and we liked each other but only knew each other superficially.

Unfortunately, just like any other bad habit, when you begin to realize that you are in the wrong, it can be very difficult to stop. I had developed a bond with him. I probably broke up with him a hundred times in my mind, knowing that although it was lawful for us to conduct ourselves the way we did, it was not spiritually good for either of us. And wouldn't you know it, we would see each other occasionally on shift. Every time he would text me and invite me over after our shift was done, knowing it was just a booty call, I still went. Even though I knew he was using me, and he knew I was using him too, we would still meet up. It was a lonely way to live. Breaking the soul tie with him was critical because once I did break it, repented to God, and asked for forgiveness, I was able to forgive myself and let it go. I also reached out to him and asked him to forgive me for using him, but he had no clue that we were doing anything wrong. He moved on to a different woman, and months later, he ended up getting an STD. Some would say that was karma putting a smackdown on him, and who am I to argue?

All I know is I repented, asked God for forgiveness, received His forgiveness, and broke the soul tie. If you are living in a similar fashion, blurring the line between purity and sensuality, bring it to God. Break the soul tie and move on. Maybe you, too, have had more than one or two booty calls, not unlike the woman at the well. However many indiscretions you have had, I am not here to judge you. God knows I am in no position to judge any woman for anything. But if that is the case in your life—you had an indiscretion, a relationship with a man you were not married to—I can say from experience that taking the first step and repenting, then asking for God's forgiveness (and accepting His forgiveness) will give you the strength you need to cut the soul tie. When you do cut it, you will find it exponentially easier to say no to that person because, trust me, when you close that door, they will try to come back again and again.

MAINSTREAM ENTERTAINMENT IS NOT YOUR FRIEND.

Never forget that Satan is here on a mission. Jesus, in John 10:10, called him a thief. He said, "The thief does not come except to steal, and to kill, and to destroy. I have come that they may have life, and that they may have it more abundantly."

Any time you open yourself up by willingly entering into an agreement with the enemy, you allow the enemy to put his foot in the door to your mind. Allowing worldly entertainment into your home that emphasizes bad behavior in an appealing way can be dangerous, and its effects can be long-lasting. Keep in mind that what we let into our spirit will eventually desensitize us to the content that we are viewing. The saying "garbage in, garbage out" is never truer than when it comes to feeding your spirit. If you feed on spiritual junk food, it will eventually destroy your moral barometer and draw you away from Christ.

Ever heard the saying "birds of the same feather flock together?" We become just like the people we hang out with. And if you are hanging out with mainstream entertainment and allowing it to have a foothold, then you are also allowing it to influence how you handle situations daily. You are in charge of the TV remote, and you get to choose what is on that screen, especially what your children are watching.

You and I will be held accountable for what we teach our kids and what we don't teach them. If you do have children, it will serve your household well to examine the things you allow your kids to take in.

ADDICTIONS CAN PLAGUE US, BUT THEY DON'T HAVE TO.

When you hear the word addiction, most people would think about addiction to drugs or maybe even alcohol. But addiction takes many shapes and forms. It could be gambling, gossiping, overspending, or even pornography. Addiction could come in the form of playing games on your tablet or computer, even watching an unsavory show on TV. Anything that takes God off the throne in your mind is an idol. Whatever the desires of your heart, God is fully able, capable, and willing to bring them into your life. But if you are seeking His blessings while participating in the enemies' activities, it is like putting a zip tie around God's hands. He cannot bless you when He is not on the throne in your mind and in your heart.

Trying to force your way by keeping that idol or addiction in the first place will drive a wedge between you and Christ. The wedge will become firmly seated between you and Christ when there is no desire in you to be free of it. Addictions are so difficult to break. I should know; I was a cigarette smoker for 15 years. The cigarettes were my addiction, my idol. And rather than keeping God on the throne, I kept the spirit of rebellion on the throne.

If you are trying to break an addiction, bring it up in prayer with the Lord, and He will reveal to you the source of the addiction. It is important you ask God this question because addiction goes far deeper than what people see on the surface. Whatever you do outwardly, it started in your heart. And remember, the heart is deceitful and desperately wicked. In Psalm 32:1–2, David wrote, "Blessed is he whose transgression is forgiven whose sin is covered. Blessed is the man to whom the Lord does not impute iniquity and in whose spirit there is no deceit."

When you get real with God about the source of the addiction, when you have given up the deceit and stopped hiding the addiction from God, He will quickly meet you in that spot. God will give you the strength and the courage you need to fight through and overcome the addiction. He will send you other believers who can come alongside you in agreement in prayer. His resources are infinite. When you petition God and ask Him to

WHEN YOU ARE TEMPTED

show you where in your heart the source of the addiction is, God will reveal it to you.

Then you're faced with a question. Do you repent when God calls you to be obedient to His voice, or do you run from Him? If you are not willing to repent and give up whatever is afflicting you, that is your choice. But if you decide that your desire to get real with God is stronger than your desire for that addiction, God will heal you completely. However long you have been living with this addiction, however self-destructive the behavior that you experienced from following that addiction, no matter how bad life has gotten, God will always be there for you. You may not be able to change the facts of your past, but you can absolutely change the facts of your future. God wants to see you set free from that addiction, from that idol. Why not make your move today to get real with Him and repent?

Here is how I pray when God brings things up that I need to resolve with Him:

> *Father God, You are the Alpha, the Omega, my God. Father, whatever it is in me that is not right with You, wherever rebellion is found in me, Father, please bring it to the front of my mind so I can see it vividly. Father, I recognize and acknowledge this issue of _____.*
>
> *I am guilty; there is no question. Father, please forgive me for my rebellion and for my participation in an activity that does not honor You.*
>
> *Create in me a new heart, O Lord, a heart that is satisfied in You and only You. In Jesus' name, Amen.*

ACKNOWLEDGEMENTS

I would like to thank these amazing women who have poured generously into my own journey of getting real with God. Ann S. and Leann S., you both witnessed it all, and loved me anyway. Brittany G., I give thanks to God for you every day, you make my heart smile. Karen S., for always keeping me grounded with your sweet southern accent, pointing me back to my Bible. Stephanie H., your 'tough love' is something I will cherish forever—thank you for always being straight with me. Thanks to all of you for your love, support, and encouragement! In the words of a very wise and honorable man, Dr. Martin Luther King Jr.: "Love is the only force capable of transforming an enemy into a friend, even if that enemy is yourself."

Made in the USA
Las Vegas, NV
16 January 2023

65702242R00094